WEST

SUPER
CATS

SUPER CATS

First published in 2010 as *Wonder Cats*

This revised edition copyright © Summersdale Publishers Ltd, 2017

With research by Caroline Goldsmith

Summersdale Publishers Ltd
46 West Street
Chichester
West Sussex
PO19 1RP
UK

www.summersdale.com

Printed and bound by CPI Group (UK) Ltd, Croydon

ISBN: 978-1-84953-998-2

Substantial discounts on bulk quantities of Summersdale books are available to corporations, professional associations and other organisations. For details contact general enquiries: telephone: +44 (0) 1243 771107, fax: +44 (0) 1243 786300 or email: enquiries@summersdale.com.

SUPER CATS

TRUE TALES
of EXTRAORDINARY FELINES

ASHLEY MORGAN

summersdale

CONTENTS

INTRODUCTION

Scientists have never been able to pinpoint when cats began to live with humans, but some now believe it could have happened as long as 12,000 years ago. Since then, they've been revered as gods and reviled as demons, but they've been our constant companions throughout.

Cats are creatures of contradiction: they are independent but loving; they are aloof but desperate for attention; they do what they want and yet they seem to know when you need them; they are energetic little acrobats and yet sleep 75 per cent of the time; they are cute and they are deadly hunters. You cannot define a cat without contradicting yourself and, despite years of scientific research into their behaviour and psychology, there are still aspects of *Felis catus* that remain a mystery to us.

Cats have been the subject of literature and songs: they have been lauded as heroes and become international media stars, and it's often said that the internet is almost entirely made of cats. For as long as cats have been with us, they have been a source of endless fascination.

In this anthology I have gathered stories of just a few of the cats who have captured our hearts and our imaginations. Here you will find tales of loyalty, compassion, love, bravery, survival and strength, as well as stories that will remind you that cats can be really, really weird. And they will show you that, even after so many years of living together, there is still much about our feline companions that we have yet to understand – and much they can still do to surprise us.

CHAPTER 1

ACTS OF HEROISM

As cats have been living with humans for centuries, they have been present during the darkest days of our history: throughout wars, natural disasters and times of great danger. They have been by our sides through it all.

Cats' heightened sense of perception, their acute hearing, their sensitive noses and perhaps a feline 'sixth sense' are all skills that they use to keep themselves out of danger. And whilst they are often thought of as being independent creatures, intent on saving themselves above all others, there are stories of cats who have used their unique feline skills to make a difference to others, sometimes changing the course of history.

In this chapter we will hear the stories of cats who put their lives at risk to save others; who detected danger when nobody else did; who stood alongside men as they fought in the bloodiest of wars; and those who remained faithful companions during the darkest times; these are the cats that can be called true heroes.

FAITH

*When St Augustine's Church in London was hit during the
dark days of the Blitz, the foresight and bravery of a little
tabby called Faith saved both her life and that of
her kitten...*

In 1936, Father Henry Ross discovered a little squatter in his
church, St Augustine's in London. It was a stray tabby who
had found her way in in search of warmth. Convinced by his
wife, Rosalind, Father Henry decided that she could stay, and
he named her Faith.

Faith soon settled in, becoming plump and sleek, and
making herself useful by catching mice. She often sat beneath
the pulpit whilst Father Henry delivered his sermons and
she had many admirers amongst the churchgoers. Faith had
found her home.

Years passed in peace at St Augustine's but the spectre of
war appeared on the horizon in 1939 and by August 1940,
London was transformed into a dark and uncertain place.
Britain was at war with Germany and every night brought
the threat of bombs upon the city. It was around this time
that Father Henry noticed that Faith was looking slightly
plumper than usual. All became clear when a tiny kitten,
white with black ears – a tom – was found in Faith's basket.
The church celebrated the joy of the new arrival and the
kitten was named Panda because of his similar colouring to
the famous panda at London Zoo.

In early September, Faith, taking Panda by the scruff of his
neck, suddenly departed the warmth of her basket for the

cold, dusty cellar of the church. Father Henry was bemused by her behaviour, wondering why she would prefer a dark, chilly cellar to her usual spot. Gently, he took the kitten back upstairs, with Faith following him, protesting loudly. Within minutes, Faith had returned with Panda to her new spot in the cellar. Having tried a number of times to convince Faith that her basket was much more comfortable for Panda than the damp cellar, Father Henry eventually decided that 'mum knew best' and helped Faith to make her little hideout under the floor of the church. He brought down her basket and some blankets, and Faith and Panda settled down, contented.

As night fell on 9 September, the air raid warnings sounded and more bombs began to fall on London. Father Henry spent the night in an air raid shelter with many other residents of the city, but when he returned to St Augustine's the next day, his worst fears were confirmed. Many buildings had been destroyed by the bombs that night and all that remained of St Augustine's was the tower. His church – his world – had been destroyed, and Faith and Panda had been inside.

Terrified for his dear cats, Father Henry began to explore the rubble, even though the tower's crumbling roof threatened to collapse over him. Ignoring the calls of nearby firemen warning him of the danger, he continued to clamber over the smoking debris, calling for Faith. Then – barely audible – he thought he heard a faint meow. Moving dust-covered timber aside, Father Henry found Faith nursing her little kitten, and she was, he said: 'singing such a song of praise and thanksgiving as I had never heard'. Faith and Panda were scooped up into safety just moments before the tower's roof collapsed.

As a civilian cat, Faith was not eligible for a PDSA Dickin Medal for Bravery but she was presented with a special silver medal by the award's founder, Maria Dickin, at a ceremony attended by the Archbishop of Canterbury. Faith's story of resilience and survival brought hope to the parishioners as they surveyed the destruction wrought on their home.

Faith returned to sit under the pulpit of St Augustine's and her photograph was placed on the chapel wall with the following inscription: FAITH: OUR DEAR LITTLE CHURCH CAT OF ST AUGUSTINE... THE BRAVEST CAT IN THE WORLD.

SIMON

A stray cat, smuggled aboard a British frigate, survived one of the most brutal sieges in military history and shows how powerful animals can be as a morale booster in the darkest times...

Seventeen-year-old George Hickinbottom was a crew member aboard the British frigate HMS *Amethyst* in 1948, when the ship was stationed in Hong Kong. One bright morning, whilst walking in the dockyards, George encountered a small feeble-looking black-and-white cat.

The cat was friendly and George couldn't imagine leaving this undernourished creature to fend for itself, so he smuggled it aboard the *Amethyst*, where it came to be named Simon.

On board the ship and with careful care from George, Simon thrived and soon set to work, killing the rats on the lower decks. When the little stowaway was eventually discovered by the captain, he was welcomed as the mascot of the ship and quickly became very popular with the rest of the men on board. Simon became a fully-fledged member of the crew.

In 1949 the *Amethyst* came under attack, as it sailed up the Yangtze River to Nanking, from the People's Liberation Army. The army laid siege to the ship, and the *Amethyst* was trapped. A long and dangerous waiting game began. This later became known in history as the Yangtze Incident.

During the early days of the siege, shelling penetrated the captain's cabin and took the life of Commander Bernard Skinner. Simon was also hit by the shrapnel and he suffered severe wounds. His crew mates rushed him to the medical staff who treated his burns and removed four pieces of shrapnel from his tiny body. They didn't expect Simon to last the night, but against all the odds, the little cat recovered and remained a regular visitor of the medical bay, where he helped to cheer up injured crew members. Many of them were just teenagers, like George, who had had to endure witnessing the deaths of their friends. Simon's presence was a powerful morale booster in those dark days.

The siege lasted for 101 days. Once Simon had recovered from his wounds, his commitment to his duties on board did not flag. He once again set to work as chief rat-catcher – a role which had become even more important, as the rats threatened to decimate the food supplies on the ship. Losing a substantial swathe of these provisions would have been catastrophic for the crew, as there was no way for them to replenish stocks whilst the ship was under siege. Simon's work was vital to the survival of every single man on board the *Amethyst*.

During the siege, news of Simon had started to spread throughout the world and by the time it ended and the *Amethyst* escaped from the Yangtze, the cat had become something of a celebrity. As the ship made its journey back to Britain, Simon was met with admirers at every port. When it finally returned to port on 1 November 1949, Simon was given a hero's welcome and was even assigned his own naval officer to deal with the thousands of pieces of fan mail that had been sent.

Sadly, Simon died shortly after his triumphant return, suffering from a viral infection caused by his earlier wounds. The little cat was given a funeral with full military honours at the PDSA Cemetery in Ilford, Essex. Posthumously, Simon was awarded the animal equivalent of the Victoria Cross for bravery, the PDSA Dickin Medal, and also recognised by the British Navy as able seaman.

At a ceremony in 2007, Commander Stuart Hett spoke about Simon's bravery: 'Simon's company and expertise as a rat-catcher were invaluable during the months we were held captive. During a terrifying time, he helped boost the morale of young soldiers, some of whom had seen their friends killed.'

CATS AT SEA

Despite their aversion to water, there are many stories of cats making their homes at sea, especially during wartime. They are valued as excellent rodent controllers, as well as morale-boosting companions.

Cats have often figured in the superstitions of sailors too. Emmy never missed a voyage on the RMS *Empress* of Ireland until one morning in 1914 when she could not be persuaded to board. Emmy watched, mournfully, as the ship sailed away without her. The next morning it crashed into another vessel, sinking and killing more than 1,000 people on board.

Another cat was also revered for his unwavering loyalty to his ship. Carlsen lived aboard the *Liberty*, which ran aground off the coast of Cornwall in 1952. Carlsen refused to abandon ship for six weeks and it was only when salvage workers arrived to take him to shore that he reluctantly left it.

Another ship's cat, U-boat, showed an uncanny sixth sense when it came to his vessel. He liked to have extended visits ashore when the boat docked at ports, sometimes disappearing for days. But every time the crew made ready to depart, U-boat would return just in time. One day he was clearly running a little late: he was spotted racing along the dock towards the ship before making a daring leap onto the deck to the delight of his crew mates. Never one to be ruffled, U-boat immediately settled down to groom himself.

GINGABURGER

Leslie Penni credits her neighbour's large ginger tomcat for saving her life when he woke her to warn her about a fire...

Leslie Penni was asleep in her home in Hawke's Bay, New Zealand, when she heard a scratching sound at the door in the early hours of the morning. Her first thought was, I've only just painted that! – she knew it had to be Gingaburger, her cousin's cat who lived in the house opposite.

Gingaburger, a big long-haired orange cat who was named for his colouring and his big belly, was a regular visitor to Leslie's house and would usually knock with his paw on her bedroom window to be let in so he could sleep on her bed. It was quite unusual for him to start scratching her door, though.

Worried for her paint job, Leslie let Gingaburger in and he quickly made his way through the house; he ignored the bedroom and went straight to the living room, where he sat decidedly in front of a cupboard that contained Leslie's water heater. He was meowing and staring at the top of it. 'He was like a stubborn child, refusing to move,' Leslie said. Flummoxed, she coaxed Gingaburger outside and went back to her bedroom.

As she settled down again, she heard a fluttering noise coming from the corner of her room, which backed onto the very cupboard that had attracted Gingaburger's attention. Standing on a chair and expecting to see a rat, Leslie was horrified to find the glowing embers of a fire that had started at the top of her water heater. Although her home was fitted with smoke alarms, they hadn't yet detected the blaze, as it had started near the ceiling, too far above them. Leslie quickly called the emergency services and escaped to safety. She soon realised that Gingaburger must have smelt the smoke and had been trying to warn her.

> *If I had woken up any later I might not be here. Gingaburger is a lovely cat and a bit of a rogue. If he was a man I would marry him, red hair and all.*

TOTO

In Italy in 1944, a little cat called Toto demonstrated an ability to predict the future and saved his owners from one of the worst natural disasters in history…

One day in March 1944, in the Italian village of San Sebastiano al Vesuvio, Gianni and his wife Irma noticed that their little cat, Toto, was behaving strangely. He was uneasy, skittish and had to be persuaded to come into the house as the sun went down. Eventually, with Toto settled inside, the couple went to bed.

Around midnight, Gianni was rudely awoken by Toto clawing at his cheek. Gianni was hurt and angry, and was about to throw the cat out of the bedroom, when Irma intervened. As Toto was usually a sweet, docile, good-natured cat, she was spooked by his strange behaviour that day and his unwarranted attack on her husband.

She persuaded Gianni that Toto was trying to tell them something. Struck by his wife's strength of feeling, he agreed with her, and the couple packed up a few things, took Toto and set out for the house of Irma's sister a short distance away.

Within an hour the town of San Sebastiano al Vesuvio was completely destroyed when Mount Vesuvius erupted unexpectedly. A fiery torrent of lava, half a mile wide, cascaded down the hillside. The neighbouring villages of Massa di Somma, Ottaviano and part of San Giorgio a Cremano were also destroyed. The effects were devastating. In San Sebastiano al Vesuvio, 30 people were killed; it could have been 32.

Could Toto predict the future? Possibly. But it's more likely that his keen feline senses were able to detect changes in the environment prior to the disaster. Scientists have noted that there are more positively charged ions in the air just before a volcanic eruption, and it is thought that cats can detect these subtle variations, as well as changes in magnetic fields. Toto couldn't have known that the volcano was about to erupt, but he knew that something wasn't right.

PREDICTING THE FUTURE

In 1979 many cat owners in California reported that their pets were acting strangely. Shortly after this there was an earthquake along the Calaveras

Fault so powerful that it shook buildings 130 miles away. The cats had predicted what hundreds of scientific instruments had failed to detect.

Cats' sensory powers are also not limited to natural events: during World War Two, many cat owners in London felt that their pets were able to predict the approach of the German bombers.

So, do cats have a sixth sense? According to scientists, a cat's secret weapon is the vomeronasal organ: a small tube of cartilage, half an inch long and situated in the roof of the animal's mouth. Cats can suck air into the tube, where they can feel, taste and smell it. This triple examination of the air around them gives cats access to much more information than a mere human nose can provide.

Cats also have excellent hearing and can perceive sounds up to 60,000 Hz (humans can only hear up to around 20,000 Hz). Thanks to their swivelling ears, cats can also hear ultrasonic noises and pinpoint a sound source to within about eight degrees. So next time you're calling your pet in for dinner and he doesn't make an appearance, it's not that he can't hear you, it's just that he's choosing not to.

MAJOR TOM

When Grant McDonald's home was in danger, it was his cat that sounded the alarm and the two best friends survived a dramatic rescue...

Grant McDonald had lived aboard his yacht, *The Osprey*, off the coast of Australia, for six years. He shared his home with his black-and-white cat, Major Tom. One morning in September 2015, Grant was woken by Major Tom repeatedly headbutting him. Grant had checked the boat a couple of times that night, as was his routine, and all was well, but something about Major Tom's behaviour seemed urgent. Grant got up and began to carry out his usual safety checks.

To his horror, Grant noted that the bow of the vessel was oddly low and discovered that the boat was rapidly taking on water. 'It was too dark and too dangerous to enter and find a leak,' Grant remembers. 'I had to make a quick decision to get the cat and get on the life raft as soon as possible.'

Grant and Major Tom huddled together on the life raft for eight hours until a Chinese vessel, *The Shi Dai 8*, diverted off its course to come to the rescue. Major Tom was lifted up onto the huge bulk carrier and Grant followed. He was taken to hospital where he was treated for shock but was soon reunited with his pet. He thanked Captain Jianbang and his crew for rescuing them but also noted that it was Major Tom who first raised the alarm.

Grant lost everything on board *The Osprey* – and has said that he and Major Tom will have to get used to living on dry land for a while – but he still has his best friend.

PUDDING

Amy Jung didn't plan on adopting a cat when she headed down to her local Humane Society, but she fell in love with Pudding and he saved her life later that day...

You just don't know when you will fall in love. And Amy Jung didn't know that she would be struck by Cupid's arrow on a visit to Wisconsin's Door County Humane Society with her son, Ethan. It was there that Amy met Pudding for the first time: a hefty 9-kilo ginger cat who stole her heart immediately. Pudding had been at the shelter with his pal Wimsey for almost a month, after their previous owner died. Not wanting to split them up, Amy took them both home with her that day.

She was pleased that both cats settled in quickly, with Pudding soon making himself very much at home, but that very night, events took a turn for the worse. Amy, who had been living with type 1 diabetes since the age of four, started to have a seizure in her sleep. Sensing that something was very wrong, Pudding leapt onto Amy's chest and began pawing her face and nipping her nose in an effort to bring her back to consciousness. She came round just long enough to try to shout to her son in the next room, but Ethan was fast asleep. So Pudding jumped down from the bed and darted into Ethan's room, pawing at him and meowing. Woken from his sleep, Ethan followed the distressed Pudding into his mother's bedroom, arriving in time to prevent her from falling into a diabetic coma. Amy believes that she wouldn't have made it through the night without Pudding's intervention – an opinion her doctors share.

Pudding is now training to be a therapy animal, and has learned to sit beside Amy and meow when her blood sugar levels are low.

Carrie Counihan, the director of the shelter who cared for Pudding before he was adopted, said: 'The fact that Pudding did what he did without knowing Amy well is just amazing to me. Pudding is now eight years old and Wimsey is three years old. Maybe, in time, he'll pick up some of Pudding's powers.'

TOM WITH TWO NAMES

The British and French armies had triumphed in the year-long Siege of Sevastopol during the Crimean War. But they were desperate for food. Enter: a tabby tomcat who became a beloved ally and a military legend...

In 1855 Captain William Gair of the 6th Dragoon Guards (the Carabiniers), a cavalry regiment of the British Army, was searching the remains of the port of Sevastopol on the Crimean Peninsula. Together with the French Army, they were the victors of a year-long siege against the Russian Army. The siege had been tough. The armies had been subjected to the hardship of a long Russian winter, their food stores and medical supplies were dwindling, and they hoped to find fresh provisions in the ruins of the port.

As they explored the largely demolished site, they came upon a large moon-eyed tabby cat sitting atop a pile of rubbish and regarding the new arrivals with curiosity. He was described as 'covered in dust and grim but serene'. He welcomed a fuss from the soldiers and did not hiss or scratch when Captain Gair picked him up. Nobody knew where this cat had come from or if he belonged to anyone but the soldiers soon realised that he must have survived the whole siege. The cat was taken back to the barracks and named Sevastopol Tom or Crimean Tom.

The soldiers noted that Tom was quite plump and had clearly had a good supply of mice and rats to keep him going during the siege. They also noted that some of the Russian soldiers who had surrendered were looking surprisingly well fed. They figured that there must be food supplies somewhere in Sevastopol – supplies that they desperately needed. The Russian soldiers were reluctant to help their captors, but the British and the French had a secret weapon: Tom.

One day a group of men followed the cat as he made his way across the port to an area that was cut off by heaps of rubble. They knew that there must be a reason why Tom was heading in that direction and they set about clearing the rubble away. To their great relief, they found what they were looking for: Tom's chosen hunting ground was awash with mice, and where there were mice there would have to be a food source. In due course, Tom led the men to all the hidden supplies.

When the time came for the soldiers to return to England, they were not going to leave Tom behind. He accompanied the men on their journey home, and became the celebrated and beloved figurehead of one of the most brutal campaigns in British military history. It was estimated that Tom was around seven or eight years old when the soldiers discovered him in Crimea. Unfortunately, he died a year after that. The men who owed so much to him felt that they wanted to commemorate his life and so, as was the fashion of the time, Tom's body was stuffed and remains on display alongside his remarkable story at the National Army Museum.

SCHNAUTZIE

Greg and Trudy Guy planned to buy a puppy from their local pet shop but a little black kitten changed their minds. What they didn't know was that this decision would, one day, save their lives...

Greg and Trudy Guy had decided to get a family pet: a puppy. So they made their way to their local pet store in Great Falls, Montana. The shop had recently taken a three-month-old kitten from a local rescue group, hoping that a customer would give her a home. When Trudy and Guy laid eyes on the tiny black kitten, it was love at first sight and they knew that they would not be going home with a dog that day. The new addition to the Guy household was christened Schnautzie.

Just six months later, on a cold night in October, Trudy was awoken at 2 a.m. by Schnautzie who was perched on her chest, patting her nose with her paw. Trudy was bemused at the cat's bizarre behaviour and went back to sleep. But Schnautzie woke her again just a few minutes later. Fortunately, Trudy didn't go back to sleep again, as she became aware of a strange hissing noise. Elbowing Greg awake, she alerted him to the odd sound, but he reassured her that it was probably a neighbour's sprinkler. Trudy was worried, though, especially when Schnautzie started sniffing insistently at the air in the bedroom. What on earth could she smell? Trudy had to investigate.

Following the source of the hiss, she entered the bathroom and the hiss soon became a roar. She realised that the gas pipe just outside had broken off above the shutoff valve, causing dangerous fumes to leak into the basement of the house.

The couple quickly grabbed Schnautzie and fled the house, calling the emergency services. Firefighters later confirmed that the family had faced a potentially deadly situation, and that the cat had woken her owners just in time.

At the time, Schnautzie was rewarded with a lot of treats, but several months later the Great Falls Animal Foundation heard about her heroics and contacted the Guys about an even bigger reward. On 10 April 2010 Schnautzie was given a Purple Paw award for bravery and became a celebrity overnight.

Greg spoke about how Schnautzie was handling all the attention and fame: 'She kind of ignores it all. They had a big dinner for her and everyone wanted to pet her. She didn't like that. She's shy around strangers.'

TINK

*Five-year-old Tink risked her own life to alert her family
to a fire in their home...*

Claire and Russell Hopkinson and their sons, Jake and Scott, were all fast asleep in their home in Shrewsbury, Shropshire, at 6 a.m., when their five-year-old cat, Tink, jumped onto Claire, waking her. Blinking in the gloom, she was horrified to find that the room was filling with smoke: there was a fire in the house. Claire and Russell got their sons out to safety and alerted the emergency services but, in the panic, Tink was nowhere to be seen. She had run off and hidden somewhere.

When the firefighters arrived, there was still no sign of Tink. Russell told them that he feared the little cat was still inside the building. One of the firemen re-entered the house to search for her and returned cradling a limp and unconscious Tink. The family braced themselves for the worst.

The Hopkinsons' daughter, Lesley, who lives nearby, said:

> *My dad thought she was dead and said it was the most heartbroken he had ever felt but the firefighters were incredible and one put an oxygen mask on her and she came round. She is a true hero; we all love her so much. Every time I see her I am reminded of what an incredible cat she is. She was utterly selfless – she could easily have got out of the house on her own but her instinct was to raise the alarm. Without her, I could have lost my family in that fire.*

Tink won the Cats Protection Hero Cat and National Cat of the Year awards in 2016.

PERCY

The Battle of the Somme has gone down in history as one of the bloodiest, but few people know that there was a cat there...

The Battle of the Somme, which took place during World War One, was intended to hasten a victory for the Allied Forces. Instead, it became one of the largest and bloodiest battles in history, ending in the wounding or death of more than one million men. What many people don't know is that a black cat called Percy was at the scene.

Percy was owned by Lieutenant Harry Drader, a Canadian who had been brought up in England. Drader was just 18 years old when he joined the Royal Northumberland Fusiliers in August 1915. When he went on to command a Mark 1 'male' tank, Percy went with him.

In 2010, the Imperial War Museum embarked on a project to restore footage filmed during the Battle of the Somme, which includes troops preparing for the Battle of Ancre, the last major British attack of the combat. The footage – filmed between September and November 1916, and titled *The Battle of the Ancre and Advance of the Tanks* – has now been fully restored and is available to view online. A clip of the film shows Lt Drader and his crew preparing to depart for battle in their tank. Drader holds Percy on his shoulders before carrying the cat into the tank with his crew. Percy stayed with Lt Drader throughout the war, and they both survived.

Percy must have been one of the few cats to see battle from such a vantage point. Lt Drader was later awarded a Military Cross for conspicuous gallantry in action.

LUCKY/UNLUCKY BLACK CAT

Whether a black cat is a bringer of good or bad luck really depends on where you are in the world. In Ancient Egypt, where cats were revered as gods, having a black cat in your home was thought to gain favours from the cat goddess, Bastet. Celtic mythology holds that the fairy Sith takes the form of a black cat and today throughout all of Britain the black cat is generally thought to denote good luck.

This wasn't always the case, though. During the Middle Ages, superstitions surrounding Satan and witchcraft led people to shun black cats. It was thought that they were demons and witches' familiars.

Black cats also feature strongly in maritime lore. If a black cat walks onto a ship and then departs, that ship is doomed to sink on its next sailing. Pirates in the eighteenth century also believed that if a black cat walked towards you, you would be brought bad luck, but if he walked away it meant good luck.

Unfortunately, some of the mystery and distrust of black cats survives to this day. Many shelters have reported that black cats are far harder to rehome than their more technicolour brothers and sisters. Cats Protection have designated 27 October as 'Black Cat Day' to celebrate the virtues of our duskiest felines and encourage people to adopt a black cat.

CHAPTER 2

PROTECTING THE PEOPLE THEY LOVE

It's often said that cats choose their humans. If a cat decides to stay then that person must be special indeed. Cats will express their love for their owners in a myriad of ways, from furry snuggles to rubbing up against legs, as well as purring and the familiar nose bump.

But some cats show true devotion and go the extra mile when their humans need them. Here are the stories of cats who have defended their owners from harm, battled predators and bullies, alerted them to danger, and brought help when it was needed most.

SYLVESTER

*A shy ginger cat called Sylvester went looking for help
the only way he could when his owner Patricia Kerr fell
into danger...*

Sylvester was a five-year-old part-Persian ginger stray cat
who had been adopted by Patricia Kerr, a 90-year-old lady
who lived alone in a small town in New Zealand. Sylvester
was a shy boy who didn't like the company of humans and
refused to be petted by anyone other than Patricia. All the
locals usually saw of Sylvester was the occasional flash of a
ginger tail as he disappeared into a bush to avoid them. So
Patricia's neighbours were taken aback when they opened
their door one morning to find Sylvester meowing loudly.

Shirley and Monte Mason wondered what had caused the
cat such distress and went over to their neighbour's door
to ring the bell. There was no answer. Shirley was worried
but thought that perhaps Patricia had gone to the shops or
for a walk. She and her husband had a family function to
attend that day so, after checking Sylvester for any signs
of injury, she decided to call on Patricia later, once she got
back home.

When they returned, Sylvester was still hanging around
and unusually vocal. The Masons also noted that Patricia
had not put her bins out for collection as she usually did on
that particular day of the week. Something must be wrong.
They rang the doorbell again and called Patricia's telephone.
No answer. Now very worried – the Masons called the
emergency services.

When the police broke in, they found poor Patricia trapped in her bath. The water had gone cold and she was hypothermic; they were just in time to save her life. Patricia was rushed to hospital and made a full recovery after a short stay.

During Patricia's rescue, Sylvester kept his usual low profile, perhaps realising that his work was done and that his owner was safe. The Masons believed that Sylvester had known that Patricia was in distress and had come to them, seeking help the only way he could. They credited him with saving Patricia's life.

THE CAT'S MEOW

Cat experts say that adult cats do not meow in the wild. Nor will a cat meow to communicate with another cat. This vocal sound is exclusively made by kittens. The 'meow' of our pets is thought to be a result of domestication, and a way of communicating with humans and getting our attention. It seems that cats have learned that certain sounds elicit particular responses from their humans and have used this to their advantage. The 'meow' is actually a purr mixed with a high-pitched cry, and studies have shown that, just like a baby's cry, humans find these calls difficult to ignore.

Karen McComb is a behavioural ecologist at the University of Sussex and discovered that cats can also manipulate us with their purrs. She was inspired to start the research by her own cat, who woke her each morning with a very insistent purring. Her research showed that cats can produce a solicitation purr, which is less annoying than a high-pitched meow but just as effective at wrestling a human from sleep so they can provide a more useful service to the cat – like filling their breakfast bowl.

JACK

Donna Dickey knew that her cat, Jack, was territorial. What she didn't realise were the lengths he would go to to defend his own backyard...

One June day in 2006, a black bear wandered into Donna Dickey's backyard in West Milford, New Jersey. Bears are not uncommon in this part of New Jersey and residents are right to be respectful of the animals which, when fully grown, weigh between 90 and 270 kilograms, and can reach lengths of 6 feet. But this particular bear didn't count on being surprised by such a territorial feline.

Suzanne Giovanetti, one of Donna's neighbours, was astonished by what she saw from her window. Donna's cat, a 7-kilogram tabby called Jack, had taken exception to the visitor to his garden and had confronted the bear. Jack's display of hissing and spitting had so disarmed the bear that it had fled and climbed almost 50 feet up a nearby tree. Having hidden amongst the branches for a full 15 minutes, the bear ventured tentatively back down, only to be chased up a second tree by a furious Jack.

Suzanne managed to take some amazing photographs of the indignant cat seated at the bottom of the tree as the bear cowered above him, before notifying her neighbour of the stand-off. It was only when Donna called Jack inside that the bear felt it was safe enough to clamber back down and make his escape into the woods.

'He doesn't want anybody in his yard,' Donna told the local newspaper.

GUARDING THEIR TERRITORY

Cats are notoriously territorial. Their territory consists of a core area where they feel secure enough to sleep, eat and play. The availability of food usually denotes how wide the cat's territory stretches, although this can vary from individual to individual. Some cats will have huge ranges, whilst others will be content to stay close to the core or home. Tomcats tend to venture out further than female cats and unneutered cats will wander even more extensively.

Cats work hard to secure their territory. They mark it out by making scratches, or with urine, to alert intruder cats that they are encroaching. The first response to trespassers is usually non-physical intimidation: hissing and spitting. As fighting is usually a last resort for cats, the animal that stands its ground usually wins. Occasionally, altercations can lead to physical fights but they are not prolonged; generally, a couple of bouts are enough to establish who is top cat.

TARA

Tara, the tabby cat, scored a big win in the eternal contest between cats and dogs, proving that felines can be fierce when something threatens their humans...

In May 2015, Roger Triantafilo uploaded to YouTube footage from his home surveillance cameras that captured hearts all over the world.

The short film shows his four-year-old son, Jeremy. Whilst playing happily with his bike in front of their home in Bakersfield, California, Jeremy is spotted by a neighbour's guard dog running loose in the street. Viewers of the video watched in horror as the dog crept up behind little Jeremy and viciously bit his leg, pulling the little boy to the ground in an unprovoked and violent attack. Within seconds, a flash of tabby grey fur appears from the bottom of the screen and hurls itself at the attacker, body-slamming the dog away from Jeremy. It is Tara, the family's cat. As the dog turns and runs away, Tara continues to defend her little human; another camera catches her hurtling after the retreating dog, making sure that he left the property, before returning to Jeremy's side. The little boy was badly hurt and needed eight stitches after the attack, but made a full recovery. Doctors said that it was quite possible that his cat saved his life that day.

Tara had adopted the Triantafilo family in 2008, when she followed them home from the park one day. When Jeremy was a newborn baby, Tara had slept close to his crib, showing an unusual bond for a creature that is usually so independent and aloof. Jeremy's mother, Erica Triantafilo, told news reporters, 'To have her, with no regard for her own life, fly at the dog to protect him [Jeremy] – I've never seen anything like that before.'

Roger's amazing footage has been viewed online more than 650,000 times and, in July 2016, the Society for the Prevention of Cruelty to Animals Los Angeles presented Tara with the 33rd annual award for the 'Hero Dog'. However, as Tara was the prize's first feline recipient, the word 'dog' was smartly removed from the trophy and the word 'cat' was etched in instead.

Tara and Jeremy continue to enjoy a close bond. Roger says, 'If Jeremy falls off his bike, she comes running. If he starts crying, she comes running.'

Little Jeremy says, 'Tara is my hero.'

HOMER

Homer didn't have the best start in life but when Gwen Cooper took a chance on him, he paid her back in love and loyalty, and didn't hesitate to defend her against an intruder...

Patricia Khuly worked as a veterinarian in Miami. A two-week-old kitten was brought into her surgery by some good Samaritans who had found him wandering the streets alone. The little black kitten had an eye infection so severe that it was life-threatening. Many vets would have reluctantly put him down but Patricia made a different choice. Although it was a decision that would save the kitten's life, it also meant that he would be blind for the rest of his life. Looking at the tiny life in her hands, Patricia somehow knew that someone would take a chance and care for him.

That special someone was Gwen Cooper. Gwen wasn't looking for another pet but when Patricia called her to tell her about the kitten, she couldn't resist meeting him. Gwen fell in love at first sight and she agreed to give him a home. She named the kitten Homer after the Greek poet, who was also blind. Homer had special needs but he was curious, fun, energetic and, above all, loving. Three years after moving into Gwen's home, Homer proved just how full of love he was for his owner.

One night, Gwen was awoken by the sound of her usually quiet, easy-going cat growling from under her bed and was confronted with everyone's nightmare: to her horror, she saw that there was an intruder in her room. 'Homer – lacking vision and therefore highly attuned to the varying sounds of my voice – knew something was horribly wrong the moment he heard my gasp of terror,' wrote Gwen, after the event. As she reacted, so did Homer. He launched his little body at the man, biting and scratching him. Shocked and disarmed by this fierce attack from such a tiny assailant, the man fled. Gwen was safe.

Homer had such an impact on Gwen's life that she wrote a book about him, which was published in 2009 with the title *Homer's Odyssey*. A percentage of the royalties go straight to animal welfare charities and Gwen continues to make donations annually to many organisations. She wrote, 'From Homer I'd learned that even the most "imperfect" of creatures is capable of loving with a deep and perfect love. All they need is someone to give them a chance.'

After spending a happy and fulfilled 16 years with Gwen, Homer passed away in 2013. The book and his legacy have meant that thousands more blind cats have been adopted. He amassed a social media following and inspired them to raise tens of thousands of dollars for the Blind Cat Rescue and Sanctuary in North Carolina, as well as for cats affected by the Egyptian revolution, the Japanese tsunami and natural disasters in the US. Gwen remembers him on her blog with a beautiful and heartfelt obituary. What Homer taught us, she says, is that 'Love isn't something you see with your eyes.'

SLINKY MALINKI

When his owner fell and risked falling into a coma, Slinky Malinki went for help and saved her life...

Janet Rawlinson lived with her cat, Slinky Malinki, in a house in Lancashire. Janet had suffered for many years from a chronic pain condition and the doctor had recently prescribed morphine. Unfortunately, Janet had a bad reaction to the medication and eventually fell into a near comatose state. This was where Slinky Malinki leapt into action.

Usually the shy and silent type, the cat began pacing up and down the neighbours' fence, meowing to get their attention. When this didn't get the response he needed, Slinky Malinki walked straight up to the house and started tapping the window. Struck by this behaviour, which was so out of character, the neighbours decided to check on Janet.

They were just in time: she was unconscious and needed immediate medical assistance. After making a full recovery, Janet commented:

> *He saved my life. Without him I might not have made it. Now he sits on the hills beyond the house and watches out for me going into the kitchen. If he doesn't see me go in for a couple of hours, he will come into the house and find me, and if I don't see him, he will tap me on the leg or the arm until I respond. He never did that until the incident. I've just*

adopted two 12-week-old kittens and he looks over them too. He is like a gentlemanly uncle. That is how he treats everybody. Both aloof and caring.

SMUDGE

When bullies threatened little Ethan Fenton, his three-year-old cat, Smudge, came to his rescue...

Five-year-old Ethan Fenton was playing with his brother Ashton at the front of their home in Doncaster, Yorkshire, when three older and much taller boys approached them. These were bullies, intent on picking on Ethan and his brother, but what they didn't know was that they would have to deal with three-year-old Smudge, the family's cat.

The boys' mother, Sharon, recalls watching from the window of their home as events unfolded and Smudge came to her sons' rescue:

> *I heard them shout Ethan's name twice but he ignored them and just put his head back down and kept playing with Ashton. And then one of the boys got in Ethan's face and said, 'Oi! Why are you ignoring me?' and pushed him over. That's when I rushed outside and saw Smudge fly out from under our car and jump on the boy's chest. I think it was shock more than anything but the boy*

> *stumbled backwards, burst into tears and then ran off.*

Smudge, a tabby-and-white cat, had come into the Fentons' lives as a ten-week-old kitten when the family were still heartbroken over the loss of their last cat. This was the first time they had witnessed Smudge's heroic alter ego. Sharon continues:

> *He has never done anything like that before but it was absolutely brilliant seeing him look out for Ethan like that. He has slept outside his bedroom keeping guard ever since it happened. I actually feel so much safer knowing Smudge is around after seeing him defend him like that. He is a big part of the family and is more of a brother to the boys than a cat.*

Smudge was awarded a Cats Protection Hero Cat award in 2014.

DUCHESS

There was a reason why Tess Guthrie's cat, Duchess, was behaving so strangely: she was trying to warn her family about a deadly threat lurking in their home...

Duchess had been behaving strangely for days and her owner, Tess Guthrie, had no idea why. She was skittish, she kept hissing and she was off her food – behaviour very unusual for her healthy little cat. Was she in pain? What was she distressed by? Tess was so concerned that she decided to call the vet and make an appointment to check on Duchess. She hoped very much that this behaviour was not a sign of illness.

Duchess lived with Tess and her two-year-old daughter, Zara, in New South Wales, Australia. She had always been a happy, gentle cat, so to see her so visibly agitated was worrying. After making the appointment to see the vet, Tess fed Duchess some food, put Zara to bed and went to sleep, hoping that she would soon find out what was wrong with her cat.

But just a few hours later, Tess was awoken by Duchess hissing in her bedroom. The cat was so aggressive and persistent that Tess put on the light and saw, to her horror, what had been agitating Duchess for so many days. A 6-foot python was coiled around the arm of her sleeping daughter.

'I couldn't believe it,' said Tess. 'At the same time I was freaking out at what I was seeing, I realised what the cat had been carrying on about for days.'

Tess credits motherly instinct, and growing up in an area where snakes are often found, for what happened next. 'I grabbed the snake's head to pry it off. I think it was startled, so it started to really bite into Zara's hand,' she remembers. 'It was wrapped around her arm three or four times and so it had a really good grip. I can't stop wondering how long it had been under my bed.' Eventually, Tess managed to unwind the snake from Zara and she threw it across the room. Mother and daughter then fled to Lismore Base Hospital, where Tess worked as a receptionist.

Both Zara and Tess were bitten by the python, but their wounds were treated and they made full recoveries. Tex Tillis, a professional snake remover, arrived the next day and took away the intruder, which was then released back into the wild, a long way away from Tess's house. Mr Tillis said that the snake had perceived the mother and child as a source of warmth. Duchess had clearly sensed the danger for days, and Tess knows that had her cat not woken her that night, it might have been too late. Duchess saved their lives.

CHAPTER 3

WORKING HARD

It is thought that cats were first made welcome in human homes because their excellent hunting skills made them useful pest controllers. Most owners will have experienced the delivery of a 'present' from their feline companions, dropped proudly at their feet or just outside a door. These gruesome gifts are said to be tributes or, as some cat behaviourists say, little admonishments to our own hunting skills, which are clearly lacking, as we cannot provide these treats for ourselves.

In this section we will not only be hearing about cats making the best of their mousing skills, but also of those who have fulfilled surprising and important roles throughout history: cats who have caught criminals, given a lifetime of service to institutions, done life-saving work, and reached the very heights of the British Establishment and the corridors of power. These cats are working hard for their living.

BEEZLEY

The real Postman Pat has been making his rounds in Lyme Regis, Dorset, with ginger-and-white cat Beezley perched in the basket of his bike...

Since the early 1980s, children all over the world have known and loved Postman Pat and his cat, Jess. Back in 2009, residents were delighted to find that life was imitating art in the town of Lyme Regis, in Dorset. Postman Terry Grinter often encountered six-year-old ginger cat Beezley on his rounds. 'I'm a cat lover so I always used to stroke him,' Terry said. One day, on a whim, he decided to lift Beezley onto the basket where he carried the letters, on his bicycle. 'I expected him to jump straight out,' said Terry. But Beezley seemed quite at home.

Soon an unusual working partnership was formed: Beezley would hop up onto Terry's basket of his own accord, accompanying him at least once or twice a week, but only if the weather was good – Beezley was not, Terry explained, a 'wet weather' feline. The cat travelled quite happily with Terry on his rounds. He often fell asleep en route and when he was disturbed from his slumber, so that the postman could reach the letters in the basket, he would give Terry an angry swipe.

Not only was Terry's mailbag a superb napping spot, but Beezley also enjoyed all the attention he got from people along the way. The pair became a familiar sight in the town. 'Don't tell me he's called Jess, because of Postman Pat's cat,' laughed Terry. 'I have to explain that he's not even mine.'

Beezley's owner is actually local resident Peter Ward, who adopted him as a kitten from his local animal shelter. Beezley might have enjoyed his days with Terry but he knew where home was. As soon as their round took him close to Peter's house, he would hop down and trot off back home – until next time.

FRED

Fred, now known as the Undercover Kitty, achieved fame when he helped the New York police to catch a man suspected of posing as a vet...

Fred was just a few months old when he was rescued by an animal shelter in New York, in 2005. As he was suffering from severe pneumonia and a collapsed lung, he was named Fred Wheezy, and his brother was called George, after the J. K. Rowling characters Fred and George Weasley from the *Harry Potter* series. Fred had had a rough start in life but his luck soon changed when he was adopted by assistant district attorney Carol Moran as part of a foster care programme. Antibiotics were administered, and steam showers and chest rubs helped Fred's condition. He soon began to thrive and even started chasing Carol's other two cats and her dogs, too. Fred was a live wire.

In 2006 the Brooklyn District Attorney's office was investigating a man called Steven Vassall, a Brooklyn resident who was suspected of posing as a veterinarian without a proper licence or training. Carrying out medical treatment on animals without the correct qualifications is a criminal offence and puts animals in incredible danger. The District Attorney just had to catch Vassall in the act. This was where Fred came in.

He was recruited as an undercover agent in the operation. His mission was to pose as a patient and expose Vassall for the fake he was. Working alongside undercover detective Stephanie Green-Jones, Fred was used as bait to ensnare the impostor. The operation was a success: Vassall was arrested and charged with unauthorised veterinary practice, criminal mischief injuring animals and petty larceny. Vassall pleaded guilty to all charges, and was sentenced to probation and mandatory psychiatric treatment.

In recognition of his contribution to keeping New York's pet population safe from the unqualified medical meddler, Fred was given a Law Enforcement Appreciation Award in May 2006 by Brooklyn District Attorney Charles J. Hynes. He was also honoured at a charity benefit later that year and presented with a Mayor's Alliance Award, which is given to remarkable animals.

Fred's career moved in a different direction after the Steven Vassall arrest. He went into training as a therapy animal, which involved being taken into classrooms to help teach children how to treat and care for animals.

Unfortunately, however, Fred was struck by a car just a few months later. Whilst playing, he had circled Carol's house and run into the street. He was killed instantly. 'I don't know what he saw, what struck him or what possessed him,' said Carol of the accident. 'He was my baby. He was very, very sweet.'

Poor Fred's life may have been short but it was full, and he will be remembered as a hero for helping to save the lives of animals who might otherwise have fallen into the clutches of Vassall.

MIKE

After dedicating his life to guarding the gates of London's famous British Museum, Mike was dubbed 'the most famous cat of the twentieth century'...

In spring 1909, Sir Ernest Wallis Budge, the Keeper of Egyptian Antiquities at the British Museum, London, was leaving his residence when a cat appeared. It was Black Jack, a frequent visitor to the museum, and he had something in his mouth. Black Jack solemnly dropped his delivery at Sir Wallis Budge's feet and walked away. He had brought a tiny kitten, who was soon named Mike.

Aside from Black Jack, there was another resident feline at the British Museum and both cats readily accepted the new arrival. Mike went on to become the most celebrated of the British Museum cats, famous for guarding the entrance throughout his 20 years of life.

Mike learned how to stalk pigeons from Black Jack and the two cats would usually spend Sunday mornings indulging in this activity. Mike would 'point' like a dog, aiming his nose towards the targets and Black Jack would gradually drive the pigeons into a corner. Each cat would seize a pigeon and carry it in to the housekeeper in exchange for a treat. The pigeons were always released back into the London skies because Mike never harmed his prey; he knew that he would have cooked meat prepared for him, which he much preferred.

Mike forged a special friendship with Sir Wallis Budge, who always ensured that the cat was cared for and fed. He was allowed to have a special corner shelf in the lodge, where he slept free of bothersome draughts. Even during the lean years of World War One, Mike did not go without.

Each day he patrolled the museum, taking up his post at the gates and monitoring the visitors. Mike did not like strangers, especially ladies. He would escape unwanted strokes by leaping up onto the top of the lodge door, which eventually was worn smooth by the frequency of his landings. Towards the end of his life he became very particular about who could feed him, and eventually only Sir Wallis Budge and the official gatekeeper were allowed this special privilege. Mike also dealt with strange dogs that sometimes wandered into the museum courtyard; they fled in terror from him.

In 1924, after 15 years of service, Mike was officially retired and declared a 'pensioner'. Sir Wallis Budge retired shortly afterwards but still visited and paid sixpence a week towards the cat's upkeep. Mike suffered from tooth decay in his later years so the three gatekeepers took it in turns to prepare tender meat and fish for him. Mike was about twenty when he passed away in 1929. Time magazine devoted two articles to this special cat and Sir Wallis Budge wrote an obituary that appeared in the Evening Standard. The Assistant Keeper in the museum's Department of Printed Books, F. C. W Hiley, also composed a poem in memorial to Mike:

Old Mike! Farewell! We all regret you,
Although you would not let us pet you;
Of cats the wisest, oldest, best cat,
This be your motto – Requiescat!

FELIX

*After five years of service at Huddersfield train station,
in Yorkshire, Felix was recognised for her hard work with
a promotion…*

As commuters arrive in the early hours to catch their trains at Huddersfield train station, they will be guaranteed the welcoming sight of a four-legged feline perched on the platform benches or blinking out of the ticket office window. This ball of black-and-white fur is Felix, the station cat. Felix has lived and worked at Huddersfield station since 2011, when she arrived as a nine-week-old kitten to keep the mouse population under control. After naming her Felix, staff discovered that 'he' was in fact a 'she', but they decided to keep the name and she has since become a stalwart member of the team, getting richly paid in cat treats and cuddles from adoring train passengers.

When a new set of ticket barriers were put up, staff soon realised that they were stopping Felix from making her usual 'mouse patrol'. A custom-made, personalised cat flap was quickly installed so that she could continue to do her work unhindered.

After five years of service, Felix earned a promotion; in 2016 she became senior pest controller and was gifted her own high-visibility jacket and TransPennine Express name badge. Staff at the station say that Felix is like one of the family and she can often be found posing for pictures on the platforms with customers or with one of her 20,000 Facebook fans (and counting!). Chris Bamford, a customer services assistant at the station, said: 'The promotion is just a nice appreciation of Felix's work. It is a reward for nearly five years of service. Her presence just brings a smile.'

STATION CATS

Felix is the latest in a long line of station cats. For example, King's Cross, in London, was home to Tizer, a rescue cat adopted by the British Transport Police. The station was overrun with rodents despite vast amounts of money being spent on pest control solutions. Soon after the arrival of PC Tizer, the station was mouse-free.

It's not just mouse-catching that makes cats such great members of the team, though. Tama, a cat who found a home at a station in Western Japan, was credited with turning the failing railway company back into a success because of the number of tourists who would visit her. Her chief role was to greet passengers at the entrance, and in 2008 she was named 'super stationmaster' and given a stationmaster's hat of her own. Tama was also a pioneer as the first female to be promoted to a managerial position within the railway company. After her death, Tama was given a Shinto-style funeral and elevated to the status of a goddess. Thousands attended to say farewell to her.

LARRY

A tabby-and-white stray cat called Larry was called up to act as 'mouser' at the most famous address in Britain and soon became a celebrity...

Larry was a stray cat in residence at Battersea Dogs and Cats Home in February 2011, when he was called up to serve his country. Larry's strong predatory instinct had been noted by the staff caring for him, and so when the call came for a champion 'mouser', they knew that only one cat could fit the bill. On 15 February, Larry moved to his new home and his new post as the first officially appointed 'Chief Mouser' at one of the most famous addresses in Britain: 10 Downing Street, the home of the British Prime Minister.

During his first year in the post, Larry became a firm favourite with staff and the public. According to the official website for Downing Street: 'Larry spends his days greeting guests to the house, inspecting security defences and testing antique furniture for napping quality.' Downing Street confirmed that Larry had made his first kill on 22 April 2011, silencing the critical voices that claimed he spent more time sleeping (and in the company of a local female cat, Maisie) than on the job. Later, in August 2012, Larry made his first public kill in front of the press gathered outside Number 10, ditching the corpse of a mouse on the lawn in front of the famous house to garner maximum publicity.

David Cameron, the Prime Minister who originally appointed the cat, has said that Larry is skittish and nervous around men, speculating that he was possibly mistreated by a male in earlier years. The exception to this seemed to be Barack Obama, President of the United States, who made a firm friend in Larry. 'Obama gave him a stroke and he was OK with Obama,' confirmed the Prime Minister. During Obama's visit to the UK in 2016, Larry was the subject of many column inches in the US press.

Larry has had to fend off many rivals for his position as top mouser. In 2012, Freya the cat moved into Number 11 with Chancellor George Osborne. Despite maintaining cordial relations with Freya, Larry came under fire for his lack of mousing activity in comparison to his neighbour's. More recently, Larry has been seen battling with the new resident of the Foreign Office, a black-and-white tomcat called Palmerston.

Other claims to fame include being the subject of a book published in 2011 and featuring on the Google Street View of Number 10, asleep next to the door.

In October 2013, when faced with the question of who would vacate Downing Street first, betting companies made Cameron the odds-on favourite to leave. Indeed, Larry outlasted David Cameron and welcomed the new Prime

Minister, Theresa May, into Number 10 in July 2016. Cabinet office staff confirmed in a press release that Larry would be retaining his position as Chief Mouser. There were concerns that he might be missing the Cameron family, but despite these difficulties, he is still odds-on to outlast Prime Minister May.

A CAT IN THE WHITE HOUSE

Abraham Lincoln, the sixteenth President of the United States, and arguably one of the most famous, was a cat lover. His wife, when asked whether her husband had a hobby, replied: 'Cats.' Towards the end of the American Civil War, Lincoln was visiting one of his generals in Virginia and made the time to adopt three orphaned kittens. These cats came to live with him at the White House, and there have been many more resident felines since. Theodore Roosevelt's cats, Slippers and Tom Quartz, came to live with him whilst he served. Calvin Coolidge took Smokey, Blackie, Timmy and Tiger with him and, more recently, Bill Clinton brought Socks and Buddy. In 2009 Socks passed away after suffering from cancer and the Clintons had his ashes transported back to Arkansas, his home.

VENKMAN, RAY, EGON AND GOZER

When Chicago-based Empirical Brewery had a rat infestation, who were they gonna call? The Rat-busters...

The staff at Empirical Brewery in Chicago had a problem: rats. They were decimating their precious grain stores and slowing down the production of their beers. The brewery had tried every method of pest control, but in a city that Animal Planet has named one of the ten worst in the world for rodents, they were facing an uphill battle. That's when four felines came to their rescue.

Chicago's Tree House Humane Society had recently started the Cats at Work Project. They took feral cats off the streets, neutered and vaccinated them, and then found businesses or private residences that needed pest controllers. As feral cats are expert hunters, they would solve their owners' problem in return for shelter and food. The cats were not pets but they could exist happily in the vicinity of humans. It meant that they were no longer living a dangerous street life and had people to look out for them.

Empirical Brewery adopted three boys – Venkman, Raymond and Egon – and a girl, Gozer, named after characters from the 1980s film *Ghostbusters*. The cats were all part of a colony found in an abandoned parking lot, so they were used to working as a team.

Since the arrival of the Rat-busters at Empirical Brewery, there have been no more rodent sightings. In fact, the only visitor has been a lost baby squirrel who was quickly rescued by the staff and released back outside the brewery. The characterful cats have also won over their colleagues, who have built them their own custom-made multi-level home near the brewing equipment, where they can relax when not on duty.

Head brewer Nevin McCown is usually first into work in the morning, so he is often the one tending to his feline colleagues. 'Whoever gets in first gets the honour of cleaning poop and taking care of the cats,' he says. As a cat owner himself, Nevin quite likes the new addition to his job description.

The cats haven't just solved the rat problem for the brewery, they've also really given them a PR boost. The cats now have a dedicated page on the Empirical Brewery website, many media outlets have published stories on the feline team, and journalism students at the local university made a short video about the cats, which was viewed more than five million times. Venkman even has his own Twitter account.

'We've definitely got more attention for the cats than the beer,' says Jim Ruffato, operations manager.

FERAL CATS AND HOW WE CAN HELP

Cats are inherently wild animals and they only become socialised through contact with humans when they are kittens. Even if the mother has been a domestic cat in the past, if she is living wild then her kittens will be incredibly difficult to tame and domesticate, and will therefore be feral. The behaviour of feral cats is so different to that of our pets that often people don't realise they are the same species. Cats Protection estimated that, in 2016 there were approximately nine million stray cats and one and a half million feral cats living in the UK. Issues arise when colonies of feral cats are left to breed unchecked, as females can have a litter that is partially weaned and already be pregnant with the next brood. Not only is this unrelenting process hard on the poor female cats, but spiraling numbers of kittens mean shortages of food and open up colonies to disease.

Many welfare groups, such as the Celia Hammond Animal Trust, have worked tirelessly to help the communities of feral cats in the UK, capturing them, neutering them and treating them for any health issues. Kittens can also be domesticated if they are caught early enough. Initiatives like the Cats at Work Project in Chicago have been groundbreaking: not only do they offer a 'green' solution to pest control, but they also take vulnerable animals off the streets and put them into environments where they can be useful and safe. Since starting the project in 2012, they have successfully placed more than 400 'working cats'.

Stray cats – cats that are lost but are not feral – can often be rehomed with the right care, even if they have 'lived rough' for a long time. Welfare organisations like Cats Protection take time to match each pet to the perfect owner, knowing that some cats will need special care and attention if they have had a particularly difficult time between homes.

CHEETO

Fearless, curious and kind, Cheeto helped over 300 lost cats reunite with their owners by fulfilling a very special role...

The Missing Pet Partnership is a service in the USA aimed at helping owners to locate their lost pets, first set up in 2001 by founder Kat Albrecht, from Washington. After helping her neighbour to find her missing cat, Kat knew that she had to assist others. She had had several years' experience as a police investigator and had worked extensively with police dogs so she knew that their keen sense of smell could be crucial in locating lost pets. Cats, especially, could stumble into holes or small spaces and find themselves stuck, but a dog could sniff them out so that they could be rescued before it was too late.

In order to train dogs to track cats, they needed a 'target'. It wasn't enough to have something that resembled or just smelled a little like a cat. Kat needed a willing feline volunteer. Enter Cheeto, a ginger-and-white tomcat, good-natured and fearless, who loved the company of dogs.

Cheeto's job was to lie quietly in a crate or a black mesh bag. He would then be hidden in woodlands, in garden waste or under the deck of a house, where he had to await the arrival of his rescuer dog. It was important that Cheeto remained quiet so that the dogs could learn to use their sense of smell rather than their hearing to locate him. This form of training also taught dogs that cats can hide in a variety of places. Their reward for finding Cheeto was a treat and being able to spend time with him, which they all loved. He worked through all seasons; his patience and good nature made him an expert at his job.

Cheeto passed away in 2014 but Missing Pet Partnership, whose work continues today, credit him with helping to rescue more than 300 missing cats.

MISTER MEANOR

When a stray cat was taken in by a police department in Illinois as their mascot, he proved himself to be a valuable member of the team and a creature full of character...

Over Memorial Day weekend of 2001, Officer Ralph Goar of the Lindenhurst Police Department in Illinois stumbled across a stray tabby cat, who seemed friendly and good-natured. Goar's boss, Chief Jack McKeever, had been thinking about getting a dog for the honorary role of department mascot, but when Ralph introduced him to the cat, it was decided that he was the perfect fit. He was named Mister Meanor – or Meanor for short.

Meanor quickly endeared himself to the police officers that made up the department and proved to have a good instinct for judging character. Officer Rebecca Labb explained:

> *If a bad guy has bonded out he yells at them the whole way down the hallway, giving them the 'what for' with a scolding meow. However, if people here need comforting, he jumps up in their lap and comforts them. He distinguishes between the good guys and the bad guys. It's amazing how he does that.*

Meanor might be the only non-human member of the team at the police department but he doesn't seem to be aware of that. He insists on drinking from the water fountain and has trained most of the officers to assist him. He will meow until he is lifted onto the platform where he can press the button to release the water and drink.

Meanor also has a mischievous side. His first misadventure occurred when he was accidentally locked in the chief's office overnight. Feeling the call of nature and being parted from his litter box meant that Meanor had no choice but, Rebecca remembers, 'that [was] when we first said that Mister Meanor committed a felony'. Another time, a visitor to the station stopped by to pay a fine and left his wallet on the counter. A cheeky Meanor pulled it through the window separating the officers and the public, and began patiently stripping him of his cash. 'The person who was here to pay a fine was not happy to pay it,' remembers Rebecca, 'but that immediately broke the ice and he started laughing. That's what Meanor brings to his colleagues at the police department – laughter and comfort. He senses when you are stressed and he'll come up and ask you for a pet. This can be a very stressful job, and he offers a great deal of stress relief.'

TOM

A cat with a love of organ music gave a lifetime of loyalty to an English church and is remembered to this day with a memorial and a poem...

In the centre of Bristol, in the UK, is one of the largest parish churches in England, St Mary Redcliffe. St Mary's doesn't have a graveyard but just outside the church, on the grass area beside the main door, visitors can see a small but unusual memorial that reads: 'The Church Cat: 1912–1927'. Whilst he is not named on the memorial, this is the final resting place of Tom.

Tom was found outside the priests' entrance to the church in 1912. Perhaps the little tabby kitten had liked the sound of the organ music; he seemed in no hurry to leave and appeared to have found the place he wanted to be. Indeed, he remained there for a further 15 years as the church cat, being cared for by the verger, Eli Richards, for much of that time.

Tom liked the church music. He would sit with the choir during rehearsals and services so frequently that it was said that he attended more church services than any member of the clergy. He particularly liked to seat himself on the stool beside the blind organist, Alfred Hollins, as he played. Tom was a friendly cat and would often make himself comfortable on the laps of members of the congregation too. The only place that was out of bounds for him was the chancel, near the altar, and he would be turfed out of there regularly.

Tom earned his keep as a mouser at the church and had quite an enviable reputation as a hunter. Whilst he often devoured his prey, he also had a habit of hiding the remains in a rather special spot. When workers removed the huge altar cross in the early 1920s for restoration purposes, they found a stash of bones and feathers big enough to fill a large bathtub. Tom had been busy!

Tom passed away in 1927, much to the heartbreak of the church staff and the congregation. In recognition of his devotion to St Mary's, he was given a grand funeral. His tiny coffin was borne to his resting place by the verger, the vicar and the church wardens, accompanied by his favourite music played on the church organ. A sonnet to his memory was written by Gilbert Croker:

> Beneath a stone in Redcliffe's churchyard lies
> What was a strange thing in God's house: a cat,
> Which was, before its very sad demise,
> Often upon the organ-stool just sat
> Listening to the music played soft and sweet,
> Or, in the organist's lap so still and warm,
> It would not 'turn a whisker' at the treat
> Of the noise changing to a pedalled storm!
> Its purpose in life was to keep from view
> Those furry creatures, lest they think a pew –
> Especially at Harvest time of year –
> To be a place that would, to them, be dear.
> Now the number of its years can be found
> To all who look within this holy ground.

CHAPTER 4

PROTECTING OTHER ANIMALS

Cats are lone creatures by preference and sometimes it can seem as though they are barely able to put up with members of their own species. But their protective instincts can be strong, and in this section there are tear-jerking examples of how some cats are prepared to risk it all to save their young.

More surprising, perhaps, are the stories where cats have decided to risk it all for animals that aren't necessarily in their immediate family. These examples highlight cats' capacity to be instinctively aware of another living creature's distress, and to treat it with the same gentle care and compassion they might show their own offspring.

SAMMY

Cats and dogs often don't get along. But one dog was lucky to have a friend in Sammy the tabby cat...

Sammy the tabby cat and Izzy the terrier mix pup lived together with their family in Toledo, Ohio. As is the way with dogs, one of Izzy's favourite pastimes was chasing Sammy, who unfortunately had no time for this canine nonsense, in an effort to convince her to play. But sometimes sibling love transcends rivalry and when Izzy ran into trouble one day, it was Sammy who stepped up to save her life.

Izzy was walking in the family's yard one afternoon when a larger, lone dog approached and began to attack her. The family, seeing the drama unfold, ran out from the house to try to save their pet but the larger dog had Izzy in its teeth, and they were horrified and helpless to stop him. That was when Sammy leapt into action. He approached the bully, puffing his little body out, causing his fur to stand on end and making himself as big as possible, whilst hissing to divert the attention away from Izzy. It worked: the bigger dog dropped her and began to chase Sammy – the race was on. Sammy shot through the yard, the attacking dog in full pursuit and, pulling his feline trump card out of the bag, the cat disappeared up into a tree. The dog was unable to follow and stood barking in frustration below.

Meanwhile, Izzy's family had had time to get her out of danger and seek help. Her injuries were life-threatening but Sammy's brave diversion meant that she was rescued just in time. Despite all the torment Izzy put him through, Sammy stepped up to save his canine friend.

CHRISTOPHER

Christopher is known as a 'guardian angel' to the staff at the veterinary clinic where he lives. He is a very special cat with a big heart...

Christopher was just three or four years old when he was hit by a car. He was found at the side of the road by a group of cyclists who kindly transported him to the Redwood Veterinary Clinic. He had a fractured pelvis and was unable to stand, but he recuperated thanks to the vets' help – they had no idea at the time just how special this cat would prove to be.

It turned out that Christopher was a stray, but rather than rehoming him it was decided that he would live at the clinic. It was then that he started to display some startling talents. The staff dubbed him a 'guardian angel' and a 'miracle kitty' because of his uncanny ability to sense when other cats needed help. Christopher would sit outside the cages of sick felines until someone let him in. 'It's weird, it's really true that he seems to understand things,' said Monica Thompson, the chief veterinarian. 'He knows when he can help. He alerts us when things aren't right about a cat.'

One day Christopher saved the life of a tiny black kitten who had come into the clinic with severe anemia.

She needed an urgent blood transfusion but the poor creature was so weak that Monica couldn't draw enough blood from her to fully determine her blood type. The vet was at a loss and running out of time, but Christopher kept jumping up on the operating table, rubbing against Monica and nuzzling the kitten. Was he trying to tell her something? She took a leap of faith and used Christopher's blood for the transfusion.

Monica didn't know it at the time but the kitten was a rare blood type which only occurs in about 25 per cent of the cat population, usually in purebreds: type B. As it turned out, Christopher was also type B and his blood transfusion saved the kitten's life; within hours, she was standing up, good as new. 'If I hadn't paid attention to Christopher, I probably would have lost the cat,' said Monica.

Christopher also has a knack for educating younger animals. He leapt into a cage with two feral kittens who were simply untouchable – hissing and growling, and did not like humans. Christopher taught them all about how to be a cat. Within a couple of weeks of being in Christopher's company and learning from him, the kittens were tame and managed to find new homes.

Monica has had people asking if they can adopt Christopher, but he is happy living at the clinic, and she knows that he serves a purpose there. He continues to help feral kittens, comfort the sick cats that come into the clinic and act as a blood donor. He truly is a little guardian angel.

SCARLETT

Scarlett was a stray cat who braved a burning building five times to rescue her litter of kittens...

On 30 March 1996 a fierce fire broke out in an abandoned garage in Brooklyn, New York. The New York City Fire Department responded to the call and quickly set about bringing the blaze under control. David Gianelli was one of the firefighters on the scene and he noticed a little tabby cat carrying a kitten away from the building. The cat returned to the building five times to carry each of her litter out of danger. David watched as she returned after her fifth trip and made a quick headcount by touching each kitten with her nose – she had saved them all. The poor cat, exhausted from her efforts and horribly injured, then collapsed. Her paws were burned, her coat was singed and her eyes were sealed shut with blisters from the heat. It was then that David realised that her little nose-to-nose count had been necessary, as she couldn't see her kittens but she could touch and smell them instead.

David quickly took the family to a veterinary clinic. The brave cat mother was called Scarlett. Unfortunately, the smallest kitten was weakened by the smoke and died of a virus, but Scarlett and the rest of her family survived and after three months were ready to be rehomed.

Scarlett's kittens were quickly found loving families: Oreo and Smokey went to live in Long Island, and inseparable siblings Samsara and Panuki were adopted by a family in Port Washington. Scarlett was given a new home by Karen

Wellen, who lived in Brooklyn and had recently lost her cat. Karen had also survived a traffic accident, which changed her perspective on life. She explained: 'The physical and emotional pain I suffered made me more compassionate, and I vowed if I ever allowed another cat in my home, it would be one with special needs.'

Scarlett certainly was exceptional. She lived happily with Karen, despite needing special care throughout her life as a result of her injuries, and died in October 2008. The North Shore Animal League, which cared for Scarlett and her kittens, created The Scarlett Award in her honour, presented to animals that have engaged in heroic acts to benefit others.

DELLA

Small birds are often a hearty meal for cats, but for Della the mothering instinct was too strong...

Ronan and Emma Lally lived on a farm in County Offaly, Ireland. They already had a large collection of animals but wanted some ducklings for their pond. So they bought some fertilised eggs, put them in their barn and eagerly awaited the birth of their new ducklings. One morning, when Ronan went to check on them, he found that they had hatched but were nowhere to be seen. As he was searching the barn, he was surprised by a cat leaping out of the hayloft. Ronan didn't know where she had come from, but he was all too aware that a resident feline hunter and missing birds would more than likely spell bad news: he feared the worst.

The couple searched the farm and eventually found one of the ducklings – but unfortunately it looked like the cat had got there first, as the small creature was dangling from her mouth. At first they thought that the bird was about to become dinner but then Emma noticed something: the cat was not forcefully holding it. In fact, she was holding the bird very gently, as if she were holding a kitten.

The couple watched in amazement as the cat returned to the barn, carrying the duckling. Following her inside, they discovered that she had created a little nest of her own and she dropped the duckling gently into it. Even more surprising was the fact that the other two ducklings were also there. The baby birds nestled under the cat as she gently put her paws around them. 'She was very content,' commented Emma. 'She was purring and she was really loving towards the ducklings.' The couple named the cat Della, then and there.

When Emma went to pet Della, she saw that this extraordinary cat had another surprise in store for them. She had given birth to three kittens just a short while before the ducklings had hatched. For a narrow window of a few hours, Della's mothering hormones were so strong that she would accept and nurture any little fluffy creature in the vicinity as if it were her own. Her natural instinct to feed on the small birds was overwhelmed by her mothering instinct.

Della went on to care for and even nurse the ducklings until they outgrew their kitten siblings. Emma and Ronan let the cat and her kittens stay, and the unusual little family lived happily alongside each other on the farm.

MOTHERING INSTINCTS

When a cat gives birth, her predatory instincts are suppressed. This is so that, when her kittens make high-pitched noises, much like many of the species she hunts, she nurtures instead of eating them. The cat will sometimes even tolerate a mouse or a rat that stumbles into her nest, when she is switched to 'mother mode'.

There are a number of stories about cats adopting outside their species. In Madaba, Jordan, a one-year-old cat called Nimra cared for seven chicks alongside her kittens, whilst in Brazil, a woman was astonished to find that her cat had seemingly given birth to a litter of kittens and puppies. In reality she had found the abandoned puppies and fostered them. This behaviour can also be found in big cats: the documentary *Heart of a Lioness* tells the story of Kamunyak, a lioness who became famous for trying to adopt at least six oryx calves.

PUSS PUSS

When Puss Puss spotted another animal in trouble, she leapt into action and got help...

Adrian Bunton and Karen Lewis of Icomb, Gloucestershire, were both gardeners. In 2003 they were working in the gardens of Cotswold District Council Chairman, Tim Royle. They had taken their pet cat – a black-and-white female called Puss Puss – with them. The couple liked to take her along on gardening jobs, as it meant she could exercise in safety whilst they worked. Puss Puss was a gentle cat who had lost her tail in an accident in early life, so she had trouble curling up and jumping. She also suffered from arthritis, but all this didn't stop her from saving an unlikely friend that day.

As Karen and Adrian worked, they were suddenly distracted by Puss Puss running towards them from where she had been patrolling by the swimming pool. Jill Royle remembers: 'She was in a very, very agitated state, meowing and calling and crying and being an utter pest and dashing back and forth between us and the pool.'

Eventually, Adrian and Karen went over to see what was going on and were shocked to find a lamb trapped under the pool cover. Its head was tangled in the straps, and they were keeping it from drowning in the water. The poor thing was panicking and trying to get free. Adrian jumped into the pool, whilst Karen rushed off to get help. Fortunately, the lamb was saved, made a full recovery and returned to its pastures. It might not have been such a happy ending without Puss Puss's quick thinking, though. 'She's a real little superstar,' said Karen.

SUNDAE

Popular culture has immortalised the notion of a brave dog alerting humans to a creature in distress, but Lori Church was surprised when her cat, Sundae, showed a similar drive to help her canine friend...

One of Lori Church's favourite places to walk her two dogs – just a few doors down from the home they shared with the two family cats – was the Iowa Elementary School grounds. One bright Sunday morning, Lori was strolling there with her dogs, who were busy exploring. The two cats had also tagged along with the little group and Lori felt very peaceful surrounded by her animals.

The quiet was soon shattered, though, when Lori noticed that one of the dogs, Tiki, had disappeared. Thinking that he must have just wandered off, she called for him again and again but there was no sign of him. It was then that one of the family cats, Sundae, started behaving very strangely. She began yowling persistently to get Lori's attention, clearly agitated. The little cat eventually led Lori to the back of the park, where she spotted the opening of a pipe. It was just small enough for Sundae to fit into and walk a few steps. Lori knew that something must be inside. Leaning down and staring into the gloom, she heard the faint but unmistakable sound of Tiki whining for help. The dog, a little larger than his feline companion, had become stuck in the pipe.

The rescue operation was not easy. Neighbours, the water department, staff from the school and eventually the Aurora Fire Department all teamed together to release poor Tiki; it took nearly eight hours. Sundae kept watch beside the pipe for the first three hours, before the Church family led her and the other animals back to the house. From there, Sundae kept vigil on the driveway until she saw Tiki return safely home. 'I would never have known that Tiki was in there at all if hadn't been for the cat,' Lori said. 'She is as much a hero as the Aurora Fire Department.'

CHAPTER 5

CATS WITH COMPASSION

Cats can offer companionship and comfort during our most trying times. The benefits of living with animals, especially cats, have been well documented, and the number of therapy cats in the UK and the US is growing every year. Cats are often able to reach out to patients suffering from debilitating physical and mental conditions in a way that humans cannot.

Many of these amazing felines don't need special training to make a difference to their humans. These stories show that cats can act instinctively to turn peoples' lives around, give them hope during the most difficult times and circumstances, and even make the difference between life and death.

FIDGE

In 2011, researchers discovered that dogs could be trained to sniff out cancer in the early stages. One cat owner found that this talent is not exclusively canine...

When Wendy Humphreys and her husband David adopted eight-week-old black-and-white kitten Fidge, she had no idea that the little cat would save her life.

Fidge settled in quickly with her new family in Wroughton, Wiltshire, but soon Wendy, who had always had cats, noticed that something was different about this pet. Every evening Fidge would jump up and perch herself right on Wendy's right breast. At first she thought that the kitten was just being playful and attentive, as all young cats are wont to do. But something about this repeated action from Fidge had an air of urgency, and it made Wendy start to wonder. She made an appointment with her doctor.

After tests, Wendy was horrified to discover a lump, and her worst fears were confirmed when it was diagnosed as breast cancer. After months of chemotherapy and an operation, Wendy was on the road to recovery, but her doctor made no bones about the fact that she had caught the cancer just in time. Wendy knows that, without Fidge, she would never have suspected anything was wrong.

> *The chemo is hard... but I am going to beat it, definitely. We have had four cats before but this is the first one that's done anything like this. She never leaves me alone. Every*

morning she jumps up and makes sure I'm all
right. David knows she has saved my life too.

MASHA

When a baby boy was abandoned in freezing
temperatures, in the stairwell of a block of flats, an unlikely
hero came to his rescue...

The mercury regularly dips below zero in Obninsk, in the
Kaluga region of Russia. The locals are used to the freezing
temperatures but, without the proper precautions, they can
be lethal. Nadezhda Makhovikova was in her flat when
she heard an urgent meowing coming from the stairwell,
which was home to local stray long-haired tabby, Masha.
Thinking that the cat might be hurt, she went to check and
was stunned to find her curled around a baby, asleep in a
cardboard box.

The little boy was aged between two and three months, and
had been in the stairwell, in freezing temperatures, for some
hours. Masha had heard the child's cries and climbed in beside
him, warming him with her long fur and licking his face.

Vera Ivanina was one of the paramedics who arrived to
take the baby boy to hospital. She remembers Masha running
after them as they carried him out to the ambulance. 'She
was so worried about where we were taking him,' she said.
'She ran right behind us, meowing.'

Already a favourite amongst residents, Masha was spoilt
with treats and food after her heroic rescue. Her little charge

was found to be in perfect health, and authorities began the search for his parents. It was almost certain that Masha's protective instincts saved his life that night.

FRANK

Robin was dealing with the hardest battle of his life when a kitten called Frank changed everything...

Robin, 38, from Romney Marsh, Kent, had just been discharged from a rehabilitation unit after having struggled for years with an addiction to alcohol.

> *I was in a very bad way when my wife decided to get this kitten. I'm the first to admit I was always a dog person and couldn't see what the fuss was about at first. But when I met Frank, my heart just melted.*

Helen's decision to bring Frank into their lives would change everything. Almost immediately, Robin and Frank became inseparable and formed a strong bond.

> *He became my number one supporter, following me about and being my constant companion. I was on a lot of medication and was very vulnerable, and Frank never left my side. With his support, I came through the other side.*

Robin knew that Frank was the inspiration he had needed to beat his addiction, so when the cat became ill, there was only one option.

> *Frank became very poorly with a twisted gut. We had no insurance and the vet's bill was going to be £2,000. My wife and I had been saving for a holiday with all the money I had not spent on alcohol. But there was never any question of what we should do – Frank saved my life and we were able to save his.*

Frank was shortlisted for a Cats Protection Purina® Better Together award in 2016.

JESSIE

Tracey and Stephen Jessop-Thompson were living in the wake of an unspeakable tragedy. But a little tortoiseshell rescue cat called Jessie was to prove a shining light in the darkness...

Tracey and Stephen Jessop-Thompson lived every parent's worst nightmare when their 18-year-old daughter, Lucy, died suddenly. She suffered a cardiac arrest as a result of an undiagnosed heart condition, and this devastating loss was the hardest thing they had ever had to deal with.

*Losing Lucy has been indescribably hard, and
I've learned that comfort comes in all sorts of
places, often where you don't expect it.*

A few months after Lucy's passing, a little tortoiseshell rescue
cat called Jessie came into Tracey and Stephen's life.

*I felt I really wanted a cat in our lives and
I felt drawn to Jessie after seeing her on the
Facebook page of a local animal charity...
Jessie really has been such an incredible help
to us; she has soothed me when the pain
has felt too much to bear, made us smile
during the darkest days and been a constant
presence in our lives. I was very depressed
when we got her but she helped bring me out
of myself a little. And in bed at night, when
the tears take over and I can't stop crying,
I will get up and Jessie will come and sit with
me. Without words, she is such an incredible
comfort at those times.*

Since Jessie came into their lives, the couple have found the
strength to get involved in the charity Cardiac Risk in the
Young, which works to reduce the number of deaths caused
by heart problems in young people. Tracey says that it's
very important to them that they do something positive in
the wake of Lucy's death. And no matter how hard the days
may be, they know they can come home to Jessie.

*She's a truly remarkable cat, and I don't
know where we would be without her.*

Jessie won the Cats Protection Outstanding Rescue Cat award in 2016.

CATS PROTECTION

Established in 1927, Cats Protection is the leading feline welfare charity in the UK and is dedicated to promoting the interests of domestic cats. The charity helps over 200,000 cats and kittens every year through their national network of over 250 volunteer-run local branches and 32 adoption centres.

Cats Protection's vision is a world where every cat is treated with kindness and understanding. The organisation has three objectives to achieve this: the first is to find good homes for cats in need. The second is to support and encourage the neutering of cats. The third is to improve people's understanding of cats and their needs. The charity regularly works with the UK Government to improve animal welfare legislation. It also hosts the annual National Cat Awards to recognise extraordinary felines, whose categories are: Hero Cat, Furr-ever Friends, Most Caring Cat, Outstanding Rescue Cat and the Purina® Better Together award.

THULA

An extraordinary little girl struck up a life-changing friendship with a remarkable little cat...

Iris Grace Halmshaw is an artist, whose beautiful paintings – reminiscent of those created by Monet – are sold to private collectors worldwide. Iris is also a five-year-old girl who has been diagnosed with autism and, as a result of her condition, doesn't speak much. Her mother, Arabella Carter-Johnson, devised the art sessions as a way of helping her daughter's concentration and she has been producing astonishing dreamlike landscapes since she was three years old.

Iris, like many others with autism, experienced a great deal of anxiety in social situations and found some days very hard, so Arabella thought that getting a therapy animal as a companion would help to calm her. They tried to introduce Iris to some horses but she wasn't interested. When they tried a dog, the little girl found his canine enthusiasm and energy a little stressful. Finally, Iris's online fans in the USA suggested that Arabella should try a Maine Coon kitten. Maine Coons are not only very intelligent, but also one of the gentlest breeds of cat. This was when Thula came into Iris's life.

It was love at first sight for both of them. The little artist named the kitten Thula after one of her favourite songs, a traditional Zulu lullaby, 'Thula Baba'. Iris doesn't fuss or pick up her kitten like many children of her age would do; their relationship is much more about constant companionship. The two of them are inseparable, with Thula often soothing Iris if she wakes in the night.

Thula was not a trained therapy cat but, for her friend Iris, she has gotten used to many things that are considered unusual for cats. She regularly walks in a harness, takes car journeys and bike rides, and she even makes the ultimate feline sacrifice by bathing with Iris, something that the little girl had previously found very stressful.

> *Thula has lowered Iris's daily anxieties and keeps her calm, but equally has the effect of encouraging her to be more social. She's been at Iris's side since she arrived and slept in her arms during her first night here. Thula's constant presence and gentle nature is having a remarkable effect upon Iris.*

Iris has even started to speak since Thula came into her life – something that doctors had warned may never happen.

PETS AS THERAPY

The UK charity Pets as Therapy (PAT) trains a variety of species to be therapy animals. These animals visit patients in hospitals, care homes, hospices, schools and day care homes around the country with registered volunteers. By providing people with the opportunity to touch and stroke a friendly animal, the visits bring comfort and companionship to individuals of all ages.

All breeds of cats and dogs can become part of the PAT team. Animals, including cats, can often be trained to help individuals with specific needs too. Many cats act as an early warning system to owners who suffer from health conditions. These animals have an extraordinary bond with their humans because they often mean the difference between life and death.

Nathan Cooper from Bournemouth suffers from epilepsy. His cat, Lilly, can sense when he is about to have a seizure and alerts his mother, Tracey. 'Lilly has a very close bond with Nathan,' Tracey explained. 'After one fit, he stopped breathing and Lilly started licking his mouth and somehow it kick-started his breathing. It's made a world of difference to Nathan's life and ours. Being able to get to him early makes a huge difference.' Scientists suspect that this uncanny skill has something to do with a cat's ability to detect biochemical scents thanks to their heightened sense of smell. They can perceive subtle changes in our body that are simply imperceptible to us.

SMOKIE

A little stray cat wandered into the lives of a grieving family in Woking, Surrey, and transformed them for the better...

Jane Leggott and her son, Stefan, 18, were grieving after the death of her husband, from cancer. Jane was particularly worried about her son, who was not dealing with the loss of his stepfather very well. It was during this sad and dark time in their lives that a little cat arrived at their door. Smokie was a stray. Jane tells their story:

> *Out of nowhere this little cat arrived on our doorstep, thin and looking rather sorry for herself. We could see she clearly had a problem with her eyes and took her to a vet, who said she had a congenital eye problem which means she can't see close up and bumps into things easily.*

Jane and Stefan took Smokie home and cared for her whilst they tried to find her owner. But after a month, no one had come forward to claim her. By this point Jane and Stefan were smitten and when the vet suggested that they take Smokie to a rehoming centre, they had other ideas – Smokie already had a home.

Stefan formed an incredibly close bond with Smokie from the start. The little cat would follow him around, never leaving his side. Stefan had been very close to his stepdad and was finding the grieving process particularly hard. Suddenly, having this little bundle of fur that needed him and was there for him made him start to see the world a little differently. Jane says:

> It's been very touching to see both Smokie
> and Stefan's lives transformed. We thought
> this little stray who kept bumping into
> things needed us – in fact, we needed her just
> as much.

Smokie won the Cats Protection Purina® Better Together Award in 2016. Organiser Kate Bunting explained, 'Stefan and Smokie's story just goes to show the mutual bond which can have a profound effect on the lives of both an owner and their cat. Smokie turned up exactly when Stefan needed her and she now finally has the loving, safe and secure home that she desperately needed.'

MR BRUTUS

In 2011 Jack McBrien's life fell apart. His marriage ended and he was dealing with crippling health problems. It was his rescue cat, Mr Brutus, who kept him going…

Jack McBrien, of Hove, remembers 2011 as the year when it all started to go wrong. His marriage ended unexpectedly and he was diagnosed with a serious condition, allodynia, which caused him to be in chronic pain. He had to give up his university course where he had been working hard to train as a social worker. Jack felt that his life had lost purpose. He fell into a deep depression and also suffered from post-traumatic stress disorder. There was only one shining light in his life during those dark days: his rescued black-and-white cat, Mr Brutus.

> *At times I have been at rock bottom and have contemplated suicide many times. The one thing that has kept me going is Mr Brutus. He has been there for me throughout the whole journey, my constant support. He is my reason for living and the reason that I battle my pain every single day. Caring for him gives me something to live for and he gives me hope for a future. He teaches me that there is beauty in such a cruel world and gives me courage to continue.*

Mr Brutus was nominated for a Cats Protection award in 2016. The organiser Kate Bunting said: 'Mr Brutus goes to show that rescue cats can bring much joy, comfort and companionship into people's lives. It's truly touching to hear what a great support he is to Jack and we hope he will inspire many more people to adopt a rescue cat.'

PRINCE SMOKEY

*It's often said that cats can detect things that we can't.
Prince Smokey certainly had a sixth sense about something
that was terribly wrong with his owner, and he alerted her
in the only way he could...*

Prince Smokey is a four-year-old cat who lives with his owner, Tina, 46, in Lichfield, Staffordshire. Tina feels that she owes her life to him. She had suffered from a few health problems and Smokey was always by her side, a constant comfort. In 2015, Tina started experiencing mild chest pains. Initially, she dismissed these as indigestion but it was a change in Smokey's behaviour that made her question her diagnosis.

> *Prince Smokey is a very loving cat and always seems to know when I'm not feeling well... [he] just wouldn't leave me alone. If I was sat down, he would start pawing at my chest, looking at me and chirruping. His behaviour was quite bizarre and it really made me think. He seemed to sense something was not right and couldn't relax.*

Tina visited her GP, who referred her straight away to the local hospital. Tests revealed that she had a stenosis in the left artery of her heart and she needed surgery to prevent a heart attack.

After I got home, Prince Smokey was back to his usual self. I have no doubt that he had a sixth sense and knew something wasn't right. Without his unusual behaviour I wouldn't have followed it up with the doctor and who knows what could have happened. He is my little angel.

Prince Smokey was shortlisted for the Hero Cat award as part of the Cats Protection National Cat Awards in 2016. Organiser Kate Bunting said, 'Prince Smokey is clearly very close to his owner and is a great example of just how insightful cats can be.'

SPIKE

During the darkest times, cats can be a source of love and support. This was true of Spike and his owner Maria…

Seven-year-old Spike is a black-and-white puss who lives with his owner, Maria, in Abergavenny, Wales. Maria was struck down quite suddenly by a rare neurological disorder called transverse myelitis, which left her paralysed: she lost control of her arms, her hands and her legs. Maria was hospitalised and during this time she missed Spike very much. After many months apart, Maria started to make a slow and difficult recovery, and she was allowed to go home but her mobility was still affected.

Coming home was tough but Spike gave me so much comfort and support. He would always come and sit with me and could see I was still myself. Spike gives me so much fight – I am desperate to be able to play with him like I once did, so every day he is my therapy. I have started getting some feeling back in my right arm and it is such a joy to be able to stroke him again.

Whenever things have been tough, I can confide in Spike and he shares my ups and downs with me. He is incredibly patient and gives me so much incentive to get better.

Spike won the Cats Protection Most Caring Cat award in 2016 for all the strength and love he has given Maria. Their relationship shows how the responsibility of caring for a cat can make all the difference to people struggling with mental or physical illness. Spike provides companionship and a sense of purpose, as well as a lot of love.

TOLDO

Toldo loved his owner so much that even when he died, he continued to show his affection...

In September 2011, Ada Iozelli buried her husband Reno in their home village of Montagnana, near Florence, in Italy. Reno was 71 years old when he died. On the day of the funeral, family members noticed that his little cat, Toldo, had followed the funeral procession all the way to Reno's grave. Toldo was a three-year-old grey-and-white tomcat who had been with his owner since he was a kitten – the two had been very close. But it wasn't until a few days later that the family realised the extent of Toldo's loyalty to his human.

The next day they found a little sprig of acacia placed on Reno's grave, and later that evening they noticed Toldo standing vigil there. The cat then became a regular visitor to the cemetery, each time bringing a little tribute to his owner. 'Sometimes he comes with me and sometimes he goes on his own,' Ada said. 'He brings little twigs, leaves, toothpicks, plastic cups... A bit of everything really. The whole town knows about him now. He loved my husband. It was something else! Now it's just me, my daughter and my son-in-law, and he's very affectionate with us too.'

PIPPA

A rescue cat with an astonishing ability has been a lifesaver more than 20 times over...

Black-and-white cat Pippa doesn't look special at first glance, but she has an amazing skill which has saved the life of her eight-year-old owner, Mia Jansa, more than 20 times. Mia was diagnosed as a type 1 diabetic at the age of six, meaning that if her blood sugar levels drop too low, she can experience a hypoglycemic episode, which could lead to a coma. It's a condition that needs careful management and can be quite unpredictable.

Pippa soon developed an amazing ability to detect when Mia's blood sugar levels were dipping. One night Mia was woken by Pippa clambering all over her and decided to test her blood sugar levels, discovering that they were dangerously low. Mia's mother, Laura, said:

> *We quickly realised she was warning us. If Mia didn't wake up then she would come to my door and meow. She comes onto the bed, walks onto my pillow and across me until I wake up. She really makes her presence felt; she won't take no for an answer. She knows it's important that I get up and help Mia.*

Since that first instance, Pippa has become Mia's watcher and frequently nudges her awake in the night if she thinks something is wrong. Pippa was adopted from the Jansas's local branch of the RSPCA after she was found abandoned in a cardboard box outside a shop. But Laura says that it's Pippa who's the real hero of the story. 'She came to the rescue really... She's one in a million, definitely.'

CHAPTER 6

SPECIAL FRIENDSHIPS

Whilst cats can be excellent companions for humans, the stories in this section prove that the paw of feline friendship can be extended to many more surprising species. These cats all seem to have one thing in common: an innate compassion for other living creatures. The old saying: 'Fighting like cats and dogs' falls by the wayside with one story, but this feline–canine friendship is the least surprising of this little collection.

DUSJA

A stray calico kitten was in search of shelter and food when she wandered into St Petersburg Zoo and made an unlikely friend...

In 2007, staff at St Petersburg Zoo were checking on Linda, their lynx kitten, when they were shocked to find she had a guest. A tiny calico kitten had somehow made her way into Linda's enclosure. The staff were worried at first: although Linda was still a kitten, a fully grown lynx is almost four times as big as the domestic cat, and they are fearsome predators. Would Linda's natural instincts show themselves? But she seemed to have taken to the brave little kitten: she was not hurting her and the two seemed to be enjoying each other's company.

The kitten was named Dusja – 'darling' in Russian – and was adopted by the zoo. Dusja continued to live with Linda in her enclosure, and the two have become inseparable as they grew up; they share toys, they groom each other and sleep curled up together. Linda is now fully grown and much bigger than her friend but she is very gentle with the cat. Staff at the zoo think that Dusja views Linda as her mother – whatever their relationship, their amazing bond shows that feline friendship is always surprising.

TIGER VS TABBY

Big cats are similar in many ways to our domestic companions. They greet each other with that familiar headbutt that your kitty will sometimes use to welcome you. Both big cats and our pet cats smell by using their mouths, and when they come across something really interesting, they open their mouths to get a better whiff. All cats have the instinct to hunt, and that little wiggle that your pet does before they pounce can be seen in big cats too. And, of course, all cats love to play.

There are some differences, though, aside from size. That cute little purr you get from your pet won't happen with big cats. The latter have a bone in their throat that domestic cats are missing – this allows them to roar but not to purr. The pupils of a domestic cat's eyes will close to a slit, whereas big cats have pupils that close to a circle, more like human eyes.

But next time you watch your pet do that little wiggle before they pounce on the toy they are playing with, look into their eyes and you will see that there is a tiger in there.

MANGO

*Although Mango always had a caring nature,
his owner was surprised when he made an unusual
choice of adoptees…*

Mango is a big ginger tom who lives with his owner and
his sister Chloe in Kentucky. He was part of a litter born
under the decking of his owner's house. Most of his siblings
were found homes, but his owner decided to keep Mango
and Chloe. Mango is a loving cat: he has a long history of
caring for foster kittens and even taking feral kittens under
his gentle paw. His owner recalls the time when Mango first
showed his caring side:

> *Before I could get his mom fixed, she had
> another litter of five. When they were old
> enough to bring inside, Mango cared for
> them. I have since fostered around six
> other feral kittens and once they are out of
> quarantine, Mango is there grooming them
> and playing with them.*

But Mango soon had two rather surprising new adoptees.
His owner continues:

> *Also, I bred Holland Lop bunnies… Mango
> jumped into their exercise pen whilst they
> were out of their cages.*

His owner posted a video online, which soon went viral. It showed Mango relaxing with the two tiny baby bunnies, gently grooming them and playing with them as if they were his kittens. It seems that Mango's caring streak makes him the perfect babysitter for any type of animal!

COCO

When Decan Anderson rescued an injured squirrel he found in his garden, it was his cat Coco who stepped up as an unusual foster parent...

When he found an injured baby red squirrel next to his building in Denmark, Decan Anderson knew that he had to try to save the little guy. The squirrel had fallen roughly four storeys from his nest and cut his chest on the way down. His mother had abandoned him for dead so Decan was his only hope. He quickly picked up the tiny creature and took him inside.

Decan's family and his cat Coco rallied around the new arrival, whom they named Tintin. Decan had adopted Coco and her brother Tiger four years earlier from a family who could no longer care for them. Decan says on his Instagram feed:

> *Tiger has always been the bad ass of the two, while Coco was the loving, caring and cuddly little princess. When Tiger would come home with a mouse or a bird, Coco would fight her brother for it; she would take it from him and care for*

> *it. Licking it, warming it like it was her*
> *own little kitten. Time went on and then*
> *four years later a miracle landed in our*
> *garden. Tintin had arrived. I knew Coco*
> *and her personality so I had no worries in*
> *my heart, when I handed her the wounded*
> *squirrel baby.*

Decan put Tintin down next to Coco, who was lounging on the floor. 'Coco immediately understood the situation,' said Decan; she started to wash and clean the squirrel, and cuddle him to warm him up.

Tintin recovered from his wounds thanks to the careful care of Decan's family and, of course, Coco. It is illegal to have wild animals as domestic pets in Denmark, but Tintin was too accustomed to humans to be released into the wild so Decan got special permission to keep him with them and he now lives happily with his new family.

Unfortunately, Coco died a year later but Decan believes that she taught her brother, Tiger, to care for Tintin like she did.

> *Tintin and Tiger bonded on a whole new*
> *level... they always greet each other with*
> *nose bumps. I have lost count of how many*
> *times Tiger has spotted and chased off*
> *hawks, other cats and, yes, even a dog to*
> *protect Tintin.*

Thousands of people now follow Tintin's adventures on Instagram – an amazing legacy for a caring, gentle cat.

KOMARI

Rescued after she was abandoned at just five months old, Komari was adopted by an unusual family which she soon made her own…

Komari is a cat but she doesn't think so. She was just five months old when she was discovered, abandoned and very sickly, by an animal shelter. This cute grey tabby soon found a caring family, but they had one concern: how would Komari settle in with her new brothers – six male ferrets – already in residence at the family home?

It turned out that Komari's new owners needn't have worried. The ferrets took to the cat as if she were one of their own. And Komari? She embraced her new family with so much gusto that she started to show behaviour that was decidedly 'ferret-ish'. Komari snuggles and plays with her brothers, and she tends to sleep with them, sardine-fashion, as is their way. She also grooms them and enjoys her meals with them. The seven animals are inseparable. The only thing that Komari finds frustrating now that she is a fully grown cat is that she can no longer fit down her brothers' tunnels during games. But one thing is for sure: Komari is perfectly happy with her ferret family.

LIBBY

Ginger tabby Libby forged an exceptional relationship with a dog named Cashew. When Cashew started to lose her sight, Libby stepped in to help in an extraordinary way...

In 1998, animal lover Terry Burns found two malnourished kittens huddling in a box in a pet shop. He took them home to the house he shared with his wife Deb and four dogs in Middleburg, Pennsylvania. The Burns weren't sure whether the kittens would survive, as they were in such a desperate state, but with love and care they thrived. Terry named the ginger tabby Libby, as she was the same colour as a brand of tinned pumpkins of the same name. Her shyer sister was called Lucy.

The cats grew up with the couple's four dogs and Libby developed a strong bond with Cashew – a yellow Labrador-Shar-Pei mix, named for the shape of her ears. Terry and Deb had picked Cashew out as a puppy from their local ASPCA centre and, when Libby came along in 1998, she was around seven years old.

Libby always liked Cashew's company but as the dog grew older and her sight started to fail her, Terry noticed that Libby would spend more and more time with her canine friend. By the time Cashew was 14 years old, she was completely blind. Libby then took it upon herself to fulfill a very special role. The two became inseparable – Libby even slept in Cashew's kennel with her. When the dog was taken for a walk, her feline friend would often follow and at home she would nuzzle Cashew's shoulder, steering her away from obstacles.

At mealtimes the cat would guide Cashew to her food and water dishes.

Libby had never received any training. She seemed to know instinctively what her friend needed and helped her without thought of reward. Without Libby it is likely that poor Cashew would have felt quite lonely and afraid in her darkening world.

When Cashew passed away, Libby was visibly bereft and, for a time, would wander in and out of the kennel, looking for her friend. Once Libby realised that Cashew was never coming back, she made a new bed for herself elsewhere in the house: she seemed to know that her work was done and no longer showed any interest in accompanying the Burns on dog walks or sleeping in the kennel. Her extraordinary friendship with Cashew shows that different species can understand each other and share loving bonds. In 2008, Libby was named Cat of the Year by the ASPCA in recognition of her selfless acts of compassion.

MUSCHI

At Berlin Zoo, an aging Asian bear found a loyal companion in the form of a stray black cat and their heartwarming friendship would last a decade...

When staff at the Berlin Zoo noticed a tiny black cat in the bear enclosure, they feared the worst. Their aging Asian bear, Maeuschen, was not known to be aggressive and, at nearly 35 years of age, she was an old girl, but surely instinct would prevail when the she saw the tiny feline? Their fears were misplaced. Where the little cat had come from was a mystery but she had found a friend in Maeuschen. The two quickly became inseparable and the cat was named Muschi.

Heiner Kloes, a member of the zoo's management, said, 'Muschi appeared from nowhere in 2000 and we decided to leave them together because they got on so well. They sunbathed together and shared meals of raw meat, dead mice, fruit and bread.' The two friends didn't have an energetic life. Maeuschen's advancing age brought a lot of health problems so their days were spent mainly eating and sleeping. But the cat embraced the lifestyle and loved to curl up next to her friend for a snooze in the sunshine.

Muschi, which means 'pussycat' in German, soon became a firm favourite of visitors to the zoo. Her unlikely friendship with Maeuschen attracted a lot of donations, which went towards the upkeep of the animals at the zoo.

Muschi and Maeuschen's relationship was tested in 2007 when the bear was temporarily moved to another cage so that her enclosure could be extended. Zoo staff found a distraught Muschi waiting outside Maeuschen's temporary cage, pining for her companion. So distressed was the cat that the staff decided to let her into the cage with her friend. 'They greeted each other, had a cuddle and were happy,' said Kloes.

Unfortunately, after years of suffering from arthritis and other health issues, Maeuschen died in 2010, bringing a sad end to one of the most extraordinary animal friendships on record. Muschi and Maeuschen's devotion to each other remains a shining example of the affection and loyalty that different species can have for each other.

TK

Tonda the orang-utan was sad after the death of her beloved partner. That was when a ginger tabby came into the picture and brought some sunshine back into her life...

Staff at Zoo World in Florida were worried. Tondalayo, their 45-year-old Sumatran orang-utan, was depressed and listless; she hadn't been herself since the death of her mate. Tonda was lonely but, due to her advancing age, introducing another orang-utan would have been difficult and unwise. It was then that the zoo's education director, Stephanie Willard, had an idea. She thought she knew the perfect companion for Tonda: a stray ginger tabby that had recently wandered into the zoo. The two were introduced and the love was instant. He was named TK, which is short for 'Tondalayo's Kitty'. The two friends are very happy: they play together and sleep together at night. Stephanie explains:

> *TK came to us and we found out very quickly that his personality was one that was very demanding, very loving, very understanding, and... he was a big rag-doll kitty. He's a very sweet cat. He's absolutely a perfect cat. He doesn't seem to grow out of his kitten stage. He still licks and rubs and purrs and loves all over her... I think it made Tonda 20 years younger. It's a maternal thing with Tonda. It's kind of like the most overprotective,*

overbearing mother there is. I'm very proud. This has worked out a lot better than I expected. She's got brighter eyes now. He's brought a lot of light to her.

CHAPTER 7

AGAINST THE ODDS

For cats, life isn't always easy. As natural explorers, they can get themselves into life-threatening scrapes, circumstances can also go against them and there's always the risk of falling into the wrong hands – hands that harm, neglect and mistreat. But a difficult start in life doesn't stop them from thriving. In this chapter we will hear the stories of cats that have beaten the odds. Either by accident or action, they have found themselves in desperate need, and yet they have endured. Animals are incapable of self-pity, they accept their lot in life and make the best of it. That is why all these tales of strength and endurance are also tales of hope.

GEMINI

When Louise Parker saved black-and-white cat Gemini, she had been horribly mistreated and was in desperate need of help. What Louise didn't know was that Gemini would also save her…

Gemini was at death's door when she was discovered by Louise Parker in Gillingham, Kent.

> *I found this little, crumpled cat lying in the snow on top of a wheelie bin, almost motionless. She was clearly very, very ill and struggling to breathe.*

Louise rushed the little cat to her local vet, where an X-ray revealed that she had a ruptured diaphragm and a collapsed lung – injuries that were consistent with being violently kicked. The vet gave the cat a 20 per cent chance of survival but Louise couldn't give up on her. Against all the odds, Gemini pulled through and Louise was able to give her a warm and safe home.

Gemini's astonishing recovery from her injuries is not the only exceptional thing about this little cat. Louise has struggled for many years with depression, and Gemini has become a steadfast friend and support to her, giving her a reason to keep trying and fighting.

> *I knew she would be a lovely pet but I had no idea how much she would help me. She*

*has completely changed my life and the way
I deal with my depression. Whenever I am
down and crying, she will come to my side
and meow and paw at me and I know I'm
not alone. She really is my rock.*

Gemini was shortlisted for the Cats Protection Purina®
Better Together Award in 2016. The organiser, Kate Bunting,
said, 'Gemini had such a tough time. It's amazing enough
that she learned to trust again after what she's been through.
But to go on to be such a close and loyal companion is truly
heart-warming.'

PURRING TO HEAL

It's widely acknowledged that cat ownership can
be very effective therapy for those suffering from
mental health issues. Cats offer companionship,
a sense of responsibility and – despite their
occasional aloofness – unconditional love. If that
wasn't enough, science has now proven that
your feline's happy purrs have healing powers.
The vibration of a cat's purr is between 20Hz
and 140Hz, which is known to be medically
therapeutic for many illnesses and conditions. A
recent survey found that cat owners are 40 per
cent less likely to suffer from a heart attack than
those who live in a feline-free house. Your cat's
purrs can also help to lower stress levels, lower

blood pressure, heal swelling and infection, and even benefit the healing of soft tissues and bones.

Nobody really knows why cats purr. Kittens do it whilst they are suckling from their mothers, and older cats tend to do it when they are relaxed and content.

BART

When he came back from the dead, Bart proved that cats really do appear to have nine lives...

In January 2015, black-and-white moggie Bart was found at the side of the road near his home in Tampa. He had been hit by a car. His owner was sure that he was dead so asked a neighbour to bury him. But five days later a matted and injured Bart reappeared, meowing for food. He had a broken jaw, a ruptured eye and tears to his face, as well as being severely dehydrated and hungry, but he was alive. Bart had presumably regained consciousness in his shallow grave and had clawed his way out, despite his injuries. His owner contacted the Humane Society of Tampa Bay and the cat was rushed in.

Bart needed extensive surgery and ongoing medical treatment: his damaged eye was removed, his jaw was wired and a temporary feeding tube inserted. His peculiar story quickly spread around the world, earning him the nickname 'The Zombie Cat'. Moved by his amazing tale of strength and survival, people donated nearly $9,000 towards Bart's medical treatment and recovery, which came at a cost of $11,000. The rest of the fee was covered by a special fund set up by the Humane Society.

Sherry Silk, executive director of the Humane Society, said, 'How many cats can crawl out of a grave, right? He deserves it… I can't even imagine how he must have felt. He's just a really wonderful, patient, loving cat.'

But the fight for Bart's life didn't end there. Originally, the Society had hoped that he could return home with his owner, but disturbing information about the cat's burial and the circumstances in which he had been kept up to the incident emerged as he recovered from his injuries. The team caring for Bart quickly decided that he would not be returning home with his original owner. In a statement the Society said: 'We are prepared to fight for the best interests of this cat. We hope the family will do the right thing and surrender Bart to our care so that we can find an appropriate environment for him to live out his life.' A lengthy legal process ensued, as the original owner fought to have his cat returned to him. 'Technically, I should have returned the cat to him,' says Sherry. 'I just made the decision as the CEO of our organisation that I couldn't in good conscience do that.' The legal battle cost the shelter around $5,000 and took 20 months.

But in September 2016 there was a resolution, when the shelter offered the original owner $5,000 for full custody of Bart and he accepted. A long-term staffer at the Humane Society who had been a foster carer for Bart in the interim signed the adoption papers immediately, saying, 'He has a little feline sister and a feline brother and they get along amazingly. I just want him to live a long, happy and quiet life.'

'This cat has a spirit like no other,' says Sherry, 'and he was determined to live.'

MINNIE

The Atkins were called to the rescue when a tiny kitten was abandoned just hours after she was born...

Linda and Trevor Atkins' house in the Dordogne area of France is home to a veritable menagerie. As well as their eight cats, two dogs and two horses, the Atkins also host up to 23 cats and kittens from the local Phoenix Association animal rescue centre, where they are dedicated volunteers. They have many tales of survival to tell but one story sticks in their minds.

One of Linda's neighbours called her one day to say that she had found a tiny kitten in her garden. She was still attached to the umbilical cord, but her mother was nowhere to be seen. The neighbour wrapped the tiny creature in a jumper and headed for Linda's house. It was there that Linda noted that it wasn't just the umbilical cord that was still attached, but part of the placenta as well. This little kitten had only just been born but was already alone and in desperate need of help. Sterilising some scissors, Linda cut the cord and began the gruelling process of hand raising the kitten.

As she weighed just 93 grams, the Atkins called her Minnie and installed her in their guest room, where Linda and Trevor took it in turns to feed her every three hours, day and night. At first they were confused as to why Minnie would sleep quietly for three hours before waking to be fed by Linda, whilst she fussed and meowed on Trevor's shifts. They soon discovered that the little kitten was being kept awake by Trevor's snoring.

For an entire month the Atkins diligently fed Minnie but she failed to gain weight. Kittens cannot be raised on cow's milk – it is not nutritious enough and can cause digestive problems. Linda knew that Minnie could be having a reaction to the powdered milk and that the best she could do was to offer full-fat goats' milk. Unfortunately, getting it involved a 50-mile round trip. But the Atkins were not put off by the distance: they were determined that Minnie would live. So the two of them began a series of repeated journeys, day after day, and Minnie was given the precious milk she so badly needed. She started to gain weight and at six weeks she weighed 311 grams: the Atkins had saved this tiny kitten's life.

At eight weeks old, Minnie was a healthy and happy little cat, and she soon found a new home with a lady in Brussels.

SCOOTER

*A cat left paraplegic as a kitten is bringing hope to others
as he rolls from room to room in his custom-made cat-cart
in his role as a therapy cat...*

In 2008, a kitten arrived at the clinic of Dr Betsy Kennon in Pittsburgh, Pennsylvania. At first he didn't seem visibly injured but Dr Kennon soon saw that the poor little thing was in shock. To her horror, she realised that he was paralysed from the waist down. With just two working legs, his future looked bleak, but Dr Kennon was not going to give up on him.

Clients of the clinic rallied round and raised over $300 to build him a customised cart made up of two wheels that cradled his back legs and a harness that strapped around his stomach. This allowed him to trot around with his two front paws and pull his wheels behind him.

The cat, who was named Scooter, soon became used to his new wheels, but he still needed special care. He was unable to use a litter box and Dr Kennon had to place a nappy on him twice a day. Dr Kennon had initially planned to find an understanding carer for Scooter, but it was not meant to be and by this point she had seen something special in the little cat. 'It dawned on me that he was a real people kind of cat, and possibly a good therapy cat,' Kennon says.

So Scooter became a regular visitor at the Harmarville Rehabilitation Hospital and other local nursing homes. He is much more than a cute distraction; to many of the patients he sees, Scooter brings hope. 'When patients see

Scooter in his wheelcart, they think: "If he can do it, so can I,"' Kennon says. She recalls one man who, after meeting Scooter, said that he felt like an idiot for ever feeling sorry for himself. 'Scooter doesn't seem aware that he has limitations,' Dr Kennon continues. 'Animals don't think like we do: "Poor me, I can't do this or I can't do that." They just deal with the hand they've been dealt.'

Scooter has done some wonderful work as a therapy cat. Dr Kennon recalls another occasion when the cat had an incredible impact on a stroke victim who was not speaking.

> We put Scooter up onto her bed and he snuggled right up to her. And don't you know, she pet him, she opened her eyes and she was talking to him. And I thought that's really cool. And when I turned around and looked, the recreational therapist and nurse were both in tears.

'He brings them a little bit of happiness,' concludes Dr Kennon, 'a little bit of joy, and a little bit of hope that things are going to get better.' Scooter was awarded the ASPCA Cat of the Year Award in 2012.

SPARTAN

A tiny orange kitten with a deformed leg arrived at a busy city shelter. The odds were stacked against him, but thanks to a caring owner and his own resilience, Spartan had a bright future...

Amy Hofer is the founder of A Pathway to Hope, a rescue and rehabilitation centre for cats and dogs based in North Jersey. She was eating her dinner one evening and browsing through messages on her phone when she saw a picture of a tiny orange kitten with bright blue eyes. The little cat had been abandoned by his owner at a city shelter and faced an even bigger struggle: he had a deformed front leg. The issue was probably caused by a birth defect but it would likely scare away potential adopters. Amy's organisation helped special needs animals, as they are less likely to find caring homes, so she quickly finished her dinner and was off. There was no way she could ignore this kitten's plight.

Amy soon brought the little cat back home with her. Unfortunately, the first discovery she made about her new charge was that he couldn't walk. As the kitten was just six weeks old, Amy figured that wherever he had spent the first few weeks of his life, he had been confined to a small space and not able to exercise. The little creature just sat back on his hind legs and waited patiently to be moved.

'We're not going to carry you,' Amy told him. Her whole family worked together to coax the cat into taking his first steps. They called him Spartan because he was small in stature but big in spirit. It was the perfect name for this little fighter.

Spartan gradually started to grow more confident and mobile, and Amy soon asked a friend, Janice Daut, to foster him whilst they looked for a permanent home. Janice, much like Amy, had felt a connection with Spartan's beseeching blue eyes. Whilst she had not been planning to foster a cat, she was unable to resist and Spartan moved in with her and her dog Norton. Janice was amused to find that Norton, a 75-lb Husky-Labrador, was terrified of the 4-lb kitten and would hide from the new arrival in Janice's bedroom.

Meanwhile, Spartan set about exploring his new territory. Two weeks after his arrival, Janice returned home to find Norton and Spartan lying side by side in her bedroom, and she knew that her dog had also fallen for the kitten – Spartan would be going nowhere. Fostering had turned into adoption and the little cat had found a home for life.

Thanks to the compassion and belief of his human carers, Spartan has found a way past his disability and a home where he is happy and safe. 'He gets around beautifully. You wouldn't know he's only got three legs,' said Janice.

CHAPTER 8

INCREDIBLE TALES OF SURVIVAL

It's often said that cats have nine lives because of their uncanny ability to escape the most perilous of situations. They are blessed with extraordinary abilities: they can run faster than Olympic sprinter Usain Bolt, can jump five times their own height and can survive falls from death-defying heights. And to add to all this, they are smart. In this chapter we will hear stories of cats who survived hurricanes, tornados, falls from dizzying heights, terrible abuse and injury, and the biggest terrorist attack in modern history. Every one of these cats is a survivor and every one is special.

PRECIOUS

When the tragedy of the 9/11 attacks in New York occurred, Precious was alone in her owner's apartment opposite the World Trade Center. The building was so badly damaged that her distraught owners thought they would never see her again...

On the morning of 11 September 2001, a house-sitter organised by cat owner D. J. Kerr was making her way to an apartment opposite the World Trade Center in New York. She was going to check on Precious, a Persian house cat who was home alone whilst her owners were away. But the house-sitter never made it to the apartment. That morning, two planes were flown into the World Trade Center in the worst terrorist attack in modern history. The windows in the apartment block where Precious was living were blown out when the Twin Towers collapsed later that morning, and the building was engulfed in metal, glass, smoke and debris. Precious's owners, D. J. Kerr and her husband, Steve, returned to find their home destroyed and declared unsafe for occupancy. With heavy hearts, they resigned themselves to never seeing their cat again.

But on 2 October something amazing happened. After reports of cries prompted rescuers to investigate, a cat was discovered on the roof of the devastated building. They managed to locate the animal, which was injured, hungry and utterly terrified. It was Precious. She had many injuries, including damage to her eyes and burns on her paws, and she had also suffered from smoke and dust inhalation.

Rescuers brought Precious to the Suffolk County SPCA where she was treated and eventually, after some sterling detective work, she was reunited with her relieved owners. Precious had survived 18 days without food in the burning rubble. Roy Gross of the Suffolk County SPCA said that, considering she was a house cat, it was astonishing that Precious had managed to survive, most likely by finding puddles of water to drink.

A year later, Precious had made a complete recovery and was living with her owners in a new apartment in Battery Park. 'She's doing great,' said D. J. Kerr. 'She likes to be around us a lot more. She's a real snuggle-bunny.' She added that Precious's amazing tale of survival gave them great joy and helped them to cope with the disaster that destroyed their home.

OSCAR – OR 'UNSINKABLE SAM'

A seafaring black cat called Oscar spent time on ships fighting on both sides of World War Two. His ability to cheat death earned him the nickname 'Unsinkable Sam'…

In 1941 World War Two was raging throughout Europe and on 18 May, the German ship *Bismarck* set sail on its first and only mission. When it sank just nine days later, after a fierce sea battle, only 118 of the 2,200-strong crew were not lost at sea. When the survivors were brought aboard the British destroyer HMS *Cossack*, the crew spotted a little black cat floating on a plank in the debris of the battle. The cat, who had been aboard the *Bismarck*, was rescued from the water and rehomed aboard the British ship. And so it was that a cat changed sides and became the mascot of the *Cossack*, where he was named Oscar.

The *Cossack* spent the next few months carrying out convoy escort duties in the Mediterranean and the North Atlantic, with Oscar on board. On one mission on 24 October 1941, the *Cossack* was severely damaged by a torpedo fired by the German submarine U-563 and 159 of the crew were killed in the explosion, which destroyed the front section of the ship. As the *Cossack* began to list under the weight of the water it was taking on, Oscar and the other survivors were transferred to the destroyer HMS *Legion*, whose crew tried in vain to tow the damaged ship back to Gibraltar. However, the weather conditions were against them and the task became impossible so on 27 October the *Cossack* sank below the waves to the west of Gibraltar.

Oscar was brought ashore, his crew mates marvelling that he had survived another shipwreck. The sailors at the base in Gibralter nicknamed him 'Unsinkable Sam'.

Oscar's next posting was aboard the aircraft carrier HMS *Ark Royal*, which, by an odd twist of fate, was one of the vessels instrumental in the sinking of the *Bismarck*. On 14 November 1941, the *Ark Royal* was hit by a torpedo – this time from the German submarine U-81 – quickly took on water and, again, efforts to tow the vessel back to Gibraltar were thwarted by the sea. As the survivors were gathered up from the debris in the water, Oscar was spotted clinging to a floating plank. He was described as 'angry but quite unharmed'.

Although the *Ark Royal* was Oscar's final mission, it wasn't his final sea journey. He and the rest of the survivors were transferred to the HMS *Lightning*, which delivered them back to shore.

Oscar spent the rest of the war on the base at Gibraltar, where he took on the role of mouse-catcher in the naval offices. After the war he was sent to a sailor's home in Belfast and lived out his days on dry land. He died in 1955.

This tenacious little feline is the only cat known to have survived three shipwrecks. A pastel portrait of *Oscar, the Bismarck's Cat* by Georgina Shaw-Baker hangs in the National Maritime Museum, Greenwich.

SASSY

When a tornado tore through Windsor, Colorado, destroying a veterinary clinic, Sassy was the only animal unaccounted for. She had to wait two hours, cowering under the rubble, before rescue came…

It was a pleasant day when Jane and Richard Matt of Windsor, Colorado, dropped off their 14-year-old cat, Sassy, at their local vet's clinic. The couple were going to their grandchild's graduation ceremony in Arizona. What they, and the majority of the residents of Windsor, did not know was that a violent storm was about to hit their hometown.

The storm on 22 May produced seven tornados and damaged more than 800 homes. Tornados aren't a regular occurrence in the region so there were no sirens. Some business owners, including the Garden Valley Veterinary Clinic where Sassy was staying, received calls from the emergency services, warning them to take shelter. However, the clinic was right in the path of the tornado so they had little time to do anything other than gather the staff and the animals in the most secure area of the building and hope for the best.

Meanwhile, the Matts received a call from their daughter Laura to tell them the news about the storm. Their immediate concern was for their home, where their granddaughter was caring for their dog. Laura assured them that both of them were fine but told them that she had some bad news. She had seen on the news that the Garden Valley Clinic had been destroyed by the tornado. The roof was gone, the walls had collapsed and the damage looked devastating.

Jane and Richard were beside themselves with worry for Sassy. They were terrified at the thought of losing the cat who had spent the last 14 years with them. But there was no way of reaching anyone at the clinic so they just had to wait for news and worry.

At first, the outlook seemed bleak. Although, miraculously, nobody had been injured at the Garden Valley Clinic, there was just one animal unaccounted for: a cat. Then later that evening, when Laura was catching up on the news, she saw an extraordinary development playing out on her television. The news footage showed the owners of the clinic Dr Rick Dumm and his wife Martie, helped by several volunteers, as they scoured and dug through the debris of the clinic, searching for the cat. It took two hours before they finally heard a faint meowing coming from under the rubble. Laura watched the footage with wonder as the rescuers pulled Sassy, dusty and frightened, from the remains of the clinic. She was safe and she was well.

Laura quickly called her parents in Arizona to tell them about the astonishing rescue. Jane and Richard sent an email to the local news channel, expressing their relief and their gratitude to the staff at the Garden Valley Clinic for not giving up on their cat. The news reporter said that Sassy's rescue was the only bit of good news he'd had to report that day.

There are plans to rebuild the Garden Valley Clinic and luckily Jane and Richard's house was undamaged by the tornados so they were able to return, along with Sassy, to their home.

SUGAR

They say cats have nine lives. Sugar used up one of hers when she survived a 19-storey fall from her apartment…

Brittney Kirk lived in a nineteenth-floor apartment in Boston with her four-year-old white cat, Sugar. It was a beautiful morning in 2012 and she decided to crack open a window so that Sugar could enjoy some fresh air whilst she was at work. But, around lunchtime, Brittney received a heart-stopping voicemail message on her phone from the local animal rescue team. They had her cat.

'There was only one way she could have gotten out,' Brittney said. 'I was really nervous to call back.' But, to everyone's great surprise, apart from some bruising to her chest, the cat was just fine.

The rescue team had tracked down Brittney using Sugar's microchip. Brian O'Connor, rescue services manager, said, 'When she told us she lived on the nineteenth floor, we were pretty blown away.' A woman on a lower storey had seen a 'white streak' race past her window and had found Sugar, who had landed on a small area of soft mulch.

It's a mystery as to how and why Sugar fell. She is deaf and has a habit of staring at objects invisible to humans, as well as chasing her tail in the early hours of the morning, but she is not an adventurous cat. Maybe it was curiosity. All that Brittney knows is that Sugar is a lucky cat. 'She's a tough little kitty,' she said.

LANDING ON THEIR FEET

Cats are fond of climbing and can often be found sitting in good vantage points to survey their territory, which has led to many reports of cats falling from great heights. However, many survive. Cats have an acute sense of balance, a very flexible backbone and no collarbone. So when they fall from a height, they are able to twist their bodies and right themselves during the fall so that they land on their feet. This is called the 'righting reflex'; it develops when a cat is around three or four weeks old and is perfected by the time they reach six or seven weeks. The 'righting reflex' is triggered by falls from as low as 30 cm. It has also been discovered that if a cat falls from a height of more than five storeys, they flatten and relax their bodies in the air, almost like a flying squirrel. This reduces drag and helps them to land with minimum impact, no matter how far they drop.

HENRY

A stray kitten lost his leg early in life but did not let his disability stop him from becoming an extraordinary cat...

Cathy Conheim and Donna Brooks were spending some leisure time at their home in the mountains of Julian, California, when their paths crossed with a stray silver tabby kitten. The poor creature had been badly injured and one of his front legs dangled uselessly from his shoulder. Cathy and Donna rushed the kitten to a vet, who confirmed their worst fears: his leg would have to be amputated or he wouldn't make it. Cathy and Donna had always thought of themselves as 'dog people' but they were understandably touched by the tiny life they held in their hands. They told the vet to do whatever it took to save his life and that they would care for the kitten until they could find him a new home. They called him Henry JM (Just Me).

As Henry started on the road to recovery, he overcame his new physical limitations and learned to get around on his three remaining legs. As Cathy and Donna watched Henry navigate his new world, dauntless and curious, they overcame their own negative feelings about felines and fell in love with him. They decided not look for a new home for Henry: he was already home.

Inspired by their cat, Cathy teamed up with writer BJ Gallagher to write *What's The Matter With Henry?* – a book that tells Henry's astonishing story of survival and conveys a powerful message: the power of love can overcome anything and we don't have to be defined by our misfortunes. The book won a special award for humane communication from the ASPCA, as well as being one of the books of the year for the Cat Writers' Association.

Copies sold have raised more than $50,000 for animal welfare organisations. Henry is now also the poster boy for the Just Me Project, a charitable foundation that works with educators, hospitals, military families and other organisations to help children who are recovering from illness and those with special needs. Henry's story of survival encourages people to overcome their disabilities, embrace life, and accept and see the beauty in the things that make us different. This is Henry's message to the world.

SCRUB

When Hurricane Katrina destroyed her home, Jennifer Noble feared that she would never see her cat, Scrub, again. But thanks to a microchip, he found his way home...

In 2005, Hurricane Katrina hit the US coast in the Gulf of Mexico, devastating the area and killing at least 1,836 people. Jennifer Noble lost her home in Biloxi, Mississippi. Her cat,

Scrub, had slipped out of the house to escape the stifling heat earlier in the day, and she feared that she would never see him again. She believed that there was no way Scrub could have survived the hurricane.

But Jennifer was in for the surprise of her life. Five years later, her telephone rang. It was a worker from the Humane Society of South Mississippi and he had a grey-and-white cat with him: Scrub. He had been living on the streets and the woman who had been feeding him had called the Humane Society when she became concerned for his health. The vet had simply scanned the cat for a microchip and found Jennifer's details.

Scrub had a few scars but was generally in good health. On his first night back home with his family, he resumed an old habit and climbed into bed with Jennifer's son. 'Scrub always slept underneath a blanket on somebody's bed,' she recalls. She also noted that Scrub, after five years of surviving by himself, had a new, wilder side to his personality. 'If he could talk, I'm sure he'd have quite a story to tell us,' said Jennifer. 'Today he still has his moments where he gets a little jumpy.'

'This is the power of microchipping. There is no other way that cat would have found its family,' said Tara High, the director of the Humane Society that reunited Scrub with his family. 'This is a very dramatic story with a wonderful ending.'

MICROCHIPS: SMALL BUT POWERFUL

When Patricia's cat, Lynx, went missing in 1997, she feared that she would never see him again. She put up posters, contacted local vets and searched for him but to no avail. Therefore, she was astonished when ten years later she was called by a Blue Cross worker claiming to have found him. Lynx was microchipped and the chips last for the lifetime of the cat, meaning that Patricia was reunited with him after a decade.

Microchipping is a short and painless procedure which involves injecting a tiny chip, the size of a grain of rice. That chip is registered with the contact details of the animal's owner and can be scanned by vets and animal welfare organisations when animals are found. The RSPCA and Cats Protection now microchip every cat that they rehome and there are over seven million animals registered on the Petlog database in the UK.

Stories like Lynx and Patricia's show how important it is to ensure that your cat is microchipped; should they ever stray too far, or get lost, microchips give them the best chance of getting back home.

CHLOE

Marion Wood's cat, Chloe, went missing whilst she was on a trip. She thought she would never see her again, but Chloe proved to be a fighter...

Marion Wood was looking forward to a trip to Vietnam with her husband in December 2014. She had made arrangements for her two cats, Honey and Chloe, to be taken care of by neighbours. Unfortunately, tragedy struck when Honey was fatally hit by a car, just weeks before the trip. Although poor Chloe missed her friend, Marion was confident that the little cat would be OK whilst she was away.

However, Marion was dismayed to receive a phone call from her neighbours just two days into her trip. Chloe had gone missing. They had searched for her and were continuing to do so but she was nowhere to be found. The last time Chloe had been seen, she had been on the roof of the house. A dark cloud hung over the rest of Marion and her husband's Vietnam trip.

When the Woods returned to their home in Bournemouth six weeks later, Marion heard a strange sound. It was faint, and it was coming from behind a sealed-up fireplace in their spare bedroom.

> *At first I thought I was just jet-lagged and imagining things but then I heard it again. I shouted for Patrick and we cut the fireplace open and found Chloe. She was half-dead: emaciated and couldn't see anything. We*

brought her downstairs and gave her some water and my neighbour Tammy Parkins, who works for a vet, agreed to take her into the vet's that morning.

Chloe was in trouble. She had lost more than half her body weight and was very weak. The vet only gave her a 50/50 chance of survival. Even though Chloe was fed every two hours around the clock over the weekend, by Monday her condition had deteriorated even further, but Marion and the staff at the veterinary clinic refused to give up on her. Chloe was a fighter. Eventually, the little cat started to show signs of improvement and finally Marion was able to take her home.

Who knows why Chloe decided to head down the chimney – perhaps she was looking for her old friend Honey? The fact that she survived for six weeks with no food or water makes her a very tough little kitty indeed.

ZOE

Zoe was cruelly abused as a kitten and, as a result, lost both her ears. But she found a home with Melissa Webb and her nine-year-old daughter, and now her story inspires and educates...

Melissa Webb decided to adopt a kitten to encourage her nine-year-old daughter Lexy in her dream of becoming a veterinarian. They visited their local animal rescue centre, Animal Rescue Kleberg, in Texas and met Zoe.

Zoe was a little tabby kitten who had a terrible start in life: the victim of unimaginable cruelty, she had been left for dead in a dumpster, with both ears sliced off. But with the care of the staff at the rescue centre, she recovered. Despite her horrific injuries, Zoe could hear just fine – she just looked a little different. For Melissa and Lexy it was love at first sight. 'We both cried because of the pain she must have endured but we knew instantly that we could give her the love she so desperately needed.'

As a result of adopting Zoe, Lexy wanted to learn more about how to prevent animal abuse. Melissa thought of a great idea to raise awareness and have more people hear about Zoe's tale of hope. They wrote a book called *Zoe the Earless Kitten*.

'We have been visiting schools to talk about Zoe and animal abuse,' Melissa explains.

> *The children love the book. We tell them what happened to Zoe and how they should never ever hurt an innocent animal, and the children vow to us to never do that. Lexy and I also stress that we didn't choose Zoe just because we felt sorry for her... We chose her because we knew that just because she had no ears didn't mean she didn't need to be loved like any other animal. We use this as an opportunity to teach children that we are all different on the outside, but we are all the same on the inside.*

Zoe is a fun and adventurous animal with more than a few quirks. Melissa says that the little cat likes being carried upside down, eating ice cream and playing dead when she's told off for stalking the family's pet bird. She also loves jumping into the bathtub when Lexy is taking a bath and then racing through the house and getting everything wet.

Melissa says that having Zoe in their lives has been a wonderful adventure. 'We love sharing Zoe's happy ending and how wonderfully she has made it through this tragedy.'

JOE

Joe was found by the side of the road one cold winter's day. His rescuer thought he had been hit by a car, but Joe had been shot 17 times in the head with a pellet gun. His story is one of survival against the odds...

Joe was in trouble when he arrived at the Sarnia and District SPCA in Ontario, Canada. The good Samaritan who had discovered him at the side of the road had thought that he had perhaps been hit by a car. In fact, something far more horrifying had happened: Joe had been shot 17 times in the head by a thug with a pellet gun. Staff at the SPCA quickly took him to an animal hospital where vets worked around the clock to save his life. The surgery was costly and the SPCA posted a call for donations on Facebook to cover Joe's bills.

The response was astonishing. People were lining up to donate towards Joe's care before the SPCA even opened, said assistant manager Alissa Scarpelli. 'They had three people at the front desk just taking phone calls. It was immediate, the response.' Workers still remember that day and talk about the outpouring of support for Joe. People were moved by his plight and appalled by the extreme act of cruelty that a human had inflicted on an innocent animal. The campaign raised more than $33,000 – more than enough to cover Joe's vet fees. The rest of the money went to a local animal shelter.

Joe underwent several operations and lost an eye in the attack but, against all the odds, he survived. He moved in with a family who built him his own fenced-in 'catio' in the garden, where he could play safely and securely in the fresh air. Meanwhile, Joe's fame was still growing. His Facebook page has more than 50,000 fans, and the founder of the page, Michelle Nicholson, says, 'He's a big star. I think I've seen fans from every country except the Vatican.'

Unfortunately, the animal cruelty charges brought against the man accused of shooting Joe were dropped because they were too difficult to prove. However, Michelle maintains that the campaign 'Justice for Joe' has been a success, as it has shone a light on animal abuse. Since the campaign for Joe, the Ontario SPCA investigated 17,000 complaints across the province in 2015 and responded to over 1,000 calls.

Joe continues to raise awareness about animal cruelty with frequent media appearances. He is also remarkably good-natured and affectionate for a cat that has suffered so horribly at the hands of humans. Photographer Jenilyn Sheppard, of Lime Hippo Pet Photography, took pictures of Joe for a feature in *Modern Cat* magazine. She described how Joe lazed around during the photoshoot and was better behaved than other pets who have posed for her. 'You wouldn't know he went through any trauma at all,' she said.

FROSTY

Frosty was found in a freezing barn in Wisconsin as a kitten. She was so cold that she couldn't move her limbs, her eyes were frozen open and she was close to death. With the help of her human rescuers, Frosty defied all the odds and fought her hardest to make a full recovery...

It was 30 December 2013 when Carol was handed a tiny frozen kitten. Her friend James had found the creature in his grandfather's barn in their home in Wisconsin. The winter was harsh and the temperatures had been below zero for many days with extreme wind chills. The ginger kitten was frozen in a 'C' shape: she wasn't moving and her eyes were wide open. But when Carol held her, she heard a faint meow. The kitten was still alive.

Given her chilly start in life, Carol named her Frosty. She wrapped the kitten in her shirt and began rubbing her whilst preparing some bedding to try to thaw her. Astonishingly, the kitten survived the night but Carol was concerned: Frosty was too thin and barely had the strength to hold her head up. She also appeared to be having difficulty breathing.

Carol rushed Frosty to the vet and was told that the kitten had pneumonia, severe frostbite on her ears and feet, a secondary respiratory infection, nerve and muscle damage, and that she was blind in one eye. The outlook for Frosty was bleak. She spent 15 days in an incubator, during which she was also diagnosed with a rare parasite. The odds stacked against her just kept getting bigger, but she was a fighter. Once the diagnosis was made, treatment could start and, slowly but surely, Frosty's condition started to improve. Eventually, the little kitten was allowed to go home with Carol. She was sent with a bronchodilator to help her recover from the respiratory infection, a lot of medication and a long schedule of follow-up appointments.

Frosty lost two inches of her tail to the frostbite, but over time the sight in her blind eye returned and she gained more strength. According to Carol, the muscle damage has not stopped Frosty from running around and playing like a typical cat, although she finds it difficult to walk in a straight line. Frosty remains on the medication and the bronchodilator but she is a happy, good-natured pet. 'Frosty and I are bonded,' Carol explained. 'She looked into my eyes that night and they said: "Please help me." I heard her. She has a strong will to live and is a very determined kitten.'

MR BISCUITS

A stray kitten who clambered into a car engine to keep warm survived horrific injuries and became a beacon of hope for other rescued cats...

On a cold morning in the East Falls neighbourhood of Philadelphia, a gentleman was driving to work when he stopped to inspect his car, as he had noticed that there was something wrong with the power steering. Imagine his surprise when he lifted the hood to find a tiny, desperate pair of eyes staring up at him from deep inside his engine. It was a kitten. The little stray had clambered in there to escape the cold temperatures of the night before and had travelled, trapped inside, as the car got hotter and hotter.

It took the rescue team a full two hours to free the kitten, and they transported him to the Metropolitan Veterinary Associates and Emergency Services. An off-duty veterinarian who specialised in treating burns rushed in, still in her pyjamas, to help the animal. The next few hours saw the kitten desperately clinging to life, even though he had burns on more than a quarter of his body, including a horrific wound to his back which suggested that he may even have caught fire during the journey.

Despite his many injuries, the kitten started to make a recovery, and that is when another organisation offered to help: The Grannie Project, based in Southeastern, Pennsylvania. The charity normally works to rehome senior animals, who often have more difficulty finding adoptive homes than their younger counterparts. Although this kitten was younger than their usual charges, they couldn't resist helping when they heard his story, and The Grannie Project slowly started nursing him back to health. They named him Mr Biscuits because he kneaded the blanket he liked to sleep on like dough. A fundraising effort started by the charity raised an astonishing $14,000 and every dollar went to pay the kitten's vet bills.

Mr Biscuits made a full recovery. A new home was swiftly found for him and he has since become a champion for The Grannie Project. He also has more than 25,000 fans on his Facebook page, which is used to help rehome cats and to encourage people to check their car engines in very cold weather for strays – just a quick tap on the hood could save a life.

CHAPTER 9

AMAZING JOURNEYS

In this chapter we will hear the stories of cats that have taken astonishing journeys, both unwittingly and voluntarily. Some travelled aboard ships that sailed to far-off lands, whereas others fought their way through dangers to get back home to the people or animals that they loved. Some fled from peril, whilst some charged into danger just to get to where they wanted to be. And some just defied stereotype and became happy travellers. Each one is extraordinary.

KUNKUSH/DIAS

Kunkush lost his family when they fled violence in Iraq as refugees. It would take an epic journey and the tireless efforts of some new friends to get him back to them...

In late 2015, a mother and her five children arrived on the beaches of Lesbos in a rubber dinghy, after having made the treacherous journey to escape the violence in Iraq. With them was a precious cargo: a basket containing their three-year-old white Turkish Van cat, Kunkush. Spooked by the journey, and in the melee of their arrival, Kunkush managed to escape from his basket and ran away to hide. The family searched for him for hours on the beach, calling and beseeching him to return, but to no avail. Kunkush was hiding and was too scared by the ordeal he had endured to come out. Although heartbroken at having brought their beloved pet so far only to lose him, the family knew that they had to move on and started for a refugee camp.

Days later a white cat appeared in a local fishing village. His fur was matted with sand, he was hungry and the local strays were not friendly to him. Fishermen took pity on him and gave him food; they named him Dias – modern Greek for 'Zeus'. It was rumoured that the cat had arrived with a refugee family but nobody knew where they were or how to locate them. The fishermen decided to take Dias to their local vet, where he was checked over and given his vaccinations, before Ashley Anderson, an American volunteer with a refugee charity, took on his cause. Ashley, along with her friends Amy Schrodes and Michelle Nhin, instigated a social media campaign to reunite Dias with his family.

A few weeks later, a foster home was found for the cat in Berlin. His new mother agreed to care for Dias until his family was found and, if that proved impossible, she agreed that he could live with her permanently. A crowdfunding page raised the €600 needed to pay for Dias's flight and, armed with his new European Union passport, the cat made the journey from Lesbos to Berlin.

In February 2016, a message was sent to the Facebook page that Ashley and her friends had set up to reunite Dias with his family. It was from a person in Norway who was certain that Dias was in fact Kunkush, the beloved pet of an Iraqi family that had recently moved in next door, and had spoken of their journey and of the loss of their beautiful white cat. Photographs were exchanged and the truth was revealed: Dias was indeed Kunkush.

Amy, Michelle and Ashley set up a virtual reunion via Skype with the family at their new home in Norway. During the call, a confused Kunkush looked behind the computer screen to try to reach them. After another online appeal for travel funds, Kunkush was soon on a plane to Norway for the last leg of his epic journey. After four months, a journey of 4,000 km and a lot of help along the way, the cat was reunited with his family. The event was filmed by Norwegian television and, upon seeing her beloved pet, Kunkush's owner wept and cried, 'Kunkush, my life.'

This story shows the unbreakable bonds that can exist between humans and animals, and also mirrors the many tales of refugees who travel through strange and dangerous lands to find safety, often relying on the kindness of strangers. Michelle Nhin wrote on the Facebook page: 'In a small way Kunkush's journey represents the plight of all who are seeking a better life. We need each other.'

TURKISH VANS: THE EXTRAORDINARY WATERPROOF CATS

The Turkish Van is a semi-long-haired breed of domestic cat that was bred in the United Kingdom from a selection of cats found in modern Turkey. They are a rare breed distinguished by 'Van' patterns, where the colour on their fur is restricted to the head and the tail, and the rest of their coat is white. They may have blue or amber eyes and some even have one eye of each colour. Turkish Vans also have one superpower that distinguishes them from other domestic cats: their coats are waterproof. In fact, Turkish Vans, a breed of cat whose origins trace back to the shores of Lake Van in Turkey, are often said to be happier around water than most other breeds of cat.

TIGGER

A lieutenant in the Royal Navy was surprised to find a furry stowaway on his car: a kitten had survived, clinging to his bumper, for a 300-mile journey...

In June 2016, Lieutenant Nick Grimmer was on his way back to his base at Royal Naval Air Station Culdrose in Cornwall. His journey had started in Birmingham and took him via Bristol and Bath, which meant that he finished the 300-mile trip late in the evening.

Upon arrival, Nick was surprised to hear a faint mewling coming from his car. He checked the boot, under the bonnet, the inside of the vehicle and underneath but could not find the source of the noise. Bemused, Nick asked some of the air engineers to help him with his investigations. Once they removed the rear bumper, the men were surprised to find a tiny grey-and-white kitten. Nick says: 'He must have had a long journey but he was remarkably unharmed. I am never late for work so I was left with no option but to take him in with me.'

The kitten was immediately christened Tigger because of his grey-and-white stripes, which were reminiscent of the helicopters at the base, known as Flying Tigers. Tigger soon made himself at home. 'The place where he has felt most comfortable is in my flying helmet,' said Nick. 'It's the only place he has been able to sleep.' The team at the base began a search for Tigger's owners but Commander Brendan Spoors commented: 'We are more than happy to adopt Tigger as a mascot; after all it's tradition for Royal Naval units to have ships' cats!'

KOSHKA

Sergeant Jesse Knott found Koshka in the war zones of Afghanistan in 2010 and knew they could not be parted again. Koshka undertook a perilous journey through some of the world's most dangerous terrain to get to his new home...

In June 2010 Afghanistan was a violent place. Torn apart by years of war, it was temporarily home to Jesse Knott, a Sergeant of the US Army. He was deployed at a US base in the Maiwand district of southern Afghanistan and, having already served on the front line in Iraq, he was no stranger to hostile environments.

Just a few days after arriving at his post, Jesse encountered a little stray cat who was apparently a regular visitor to the base. The cat was friendly but wary, and Jesse thought he was perhaps being mistreated, as he often showed up with paint on his fur or cuts on his back. When the cat arrived one day with a badly injured paw, Jesse knew he had to help him: he treated the injury and the two started a friendship. Jesse named him Koshka, which is Russian for cat.

Jesse had a small office where he found a space for Koshka. In the middle of the violence of war, he said that the cat became a reminder of normal life back home. 'You lose faith in a lot,' Jesse said, 'but sometimes it's the smallest things that bring you back.'

Jesse faced his darkest time in December 2010. A suicide bomb attack took the lives of two of his close friends and injured many others. 'I was so devastated that I lost all hope.

Two of my friends were taken away,' he said. Jesse was in the depths of despair, when Koshka crept over to him. 'I had tears in my eyes,' he said.

> *He locked eyes with me, reached out with his paw and pressed it to my lips, then climbed down and into my lap, curled up and shared the moment with me. I'd lost all hope in myself; I'd lost faith. Then all of a sudden this cat came over and it was like, 'Hey, you're you.'*

Jesse realised in that moment that he couldn't leave Koshka behind: he had to keep the little cat safe. 'He pulled me out of one of my darkest times, so I had to pull him out of one of his darkest places.'

Jesse was due to be redeployed and time was running out to ensure Koshka's future so he contacted the Afghan Stray Animal League; they agreed to take the cat and arrange his trip to America, where he could live with Jesse. But there was a problem: the ASAL shelter was in Kabul, halfway across the country. Jesse had to find a way to get Koshka there safely but he could not leave his post. Help came in the form of a brave local translator who was working with the US Army. He was taking leave to visit family in Kabul and agreed to take Koshka with him. Translating was a dangerous job in Afghanistan and it was a perilous journey: if the Taliban had intercepted him at one of their many checkpoints in the country, he and Koshka would almost certainly have been killed.

Jesse waited for days to receive some news. Finally, it arrived. Koshka had made it to Kabul and the safety of the shelter. The cat was given his shots and his papers, and travel arrangements were organised by the staff there. Koshka's epic journey ended with a flight that took him from Kabul to Islamabad in Pakistan, then via Europe to New York and finally on to Portland, Oregon. The cost was nearly $3,000, which was raised by Jesse's friends and family, but there's no doubt that it was worth every cent. 'He was my saving grace,' Jesse said. 'He kept me alive through that tour. Sometimes we save an animal. Sometimes an animal saves us.'

LUIGI

A Scottish Fold kitten made an unlikely friend in a Pug dog and went on an extraordinary journey with his family...

When Sebastian Smetham bought a seven-week-old Scottish Fold kitten for his partner Finn, he had no idea how it would change their lives. Sebastian and Finn lived with their six-year-old Pug dog, Bandito, and the three welcomed the little kitten, whom they named Luigi, into their home. Luigi and Bandito became firm friends immediately. Sebastian says that they were inseparable.

It was the arrival of Luigi that made Sebastian and Finn re-evaluate their lives.

> *When Luigi arrived, he seemed to take charge. It was him and Bandito who led us on this journey to find a better life for them and us. Which we did.*

Sebastian and Finn packed their bags, bought a dog trolley and a tent, and set off on a 750-kilometre journey, walking across Northern Spain on the Camino de Santiago. The trip took three months – Luigi and Bandito went with them.

Anyone who understands cats knows that they are incredibly territorial creatures. They prefer to stay on their home turf, spend a great deal of energy carving out their territory and are highly sensitive to change, so some might have scoffed at Sebastian and Finn's idea. But they knew that Luigi was not an ordinary cat.

Luigi took to the new lifestyle straight away. He was happy to travel in the trolley, which became his safe place and his base throughout the journey. Often the couple would also walk along with their cat lounging on top of one of their rucksacks and their dog on the other.

Luigi slept in the tent each night with Sebastian, Finn and Bandito. Having set off on the journey as a very young cat, he had plenty of growing up to do, and Sebastian noted how he learned a lot by climbing trees and hunting. Luigi was even neutered along the way, once he reached the proper age, and the family stayed in a campsite for four days whilst he recovered after the procedure. Sebastian noticed that Luigi has a real affinity with nature and the outdoors, and prefers to play with leaves or chase insects rather than any of the cat toys they bought him.

The trip was life-changing for Sebastian and Finn in more ways than one. Luigi and Bandito, known as 'Pug and Cat', now have their own Instagram account and Facebook pages, with thousands of followers. Their owners are working on a book about their journey together and their pets' amazing relationship.

It was Luigi and Bandito's relationship
that made it possible. They are inseparable
and one without the other would never
have worked. They look after each other
and also fight like brothers – or like cats
and dogs!

THE FIRST CAT IN SPACE

Cats have made some incredible journeys but perhaps none as amazing as Félicette. On 18 October 1963, the French Centre d'Enseignement et de Recherches de Médecine Aéronautique (CERMA) launched a Veronique AGI sounding rocket into space. On board was Félicette. She had electrodes implanted into her brain that recorded her neural impulses and transmitted them back to Earth for biological research. The cat didn't go into orbit, but she travelled some 100 miles into space on a 15-minute flight before the capsule separated from the rocket and made the descent back to Earth.

WILLOW

When a small calico house cat went missing from her home in Boulder, Colorado, nobody expected her to turn up in New York City, more than 1,600 miles away...

Willow, a small calico cat, lived in Boulder, Colorado, with her family: Jamie and Chris Squires, their children and their dog. Jamie described her as 'a really cool cat, really sweet' and the family were devastated when Willow went missing after a building contractor accidentally left a door open.

The Squires searched for her, put up posters around their town and posted notices on Craigslist but nobody had seen Willow. As the family lived in the heart of the Rocky Mountains, which is not safe territory for a little house cat, they feared the worst. Jamie said, 'To be honest there are tons of coyotes around here and owls. She was just a little thing, five and a half pounds.' The Squires consoled their heartbroken children and resigned themselves to the fact that Willow was gone.

It was five years later, in 2011, that Jamie was astounded to receive a call from an animal shelter in New York City, more than 1,600 miles away. They had found a cat on East 20th Street, Manhattan, and had been able to scan her microchip. 'All our pets are microchipped,' Jamie said. 'If I could microchip my kids, I would.' The family had since moved around ten miles from the house they had shared with Willow but had kept their address up to date on the National Microchip Registration Database, which meant that the animal shelter had been able to trace them and reunite them with their lost pet.

Chris and Jamie decided not to tell their two eldest children about the discovery until they were sure that it was their cat but when they were sent a picture by the shelter, there was no doubt. 'It was Willow,' says Jamie. Their two eldest children, who remembered Willow, were delighted to have found her. When he saw her photograph, their youngest child, just three, commented, 'She's a pretty cat.'

Willow was in good health and weighed 7 lb. The Squires were sure that after her time in the city she would have a bit of a 'New York' state of mind but she is still very gentle and well mannered. There are no clues about her trip or how she ended up so far away from home. That is a secret that Willow is keeping to herself.

JESSIE

Cats have excellent homing instincts – but Jessie astonished her owners when she walked 3,000 km to return home to her brother Jack...

Sheree Gale lived in a farmhouse in Ungarra, South Australia, with her two tabby cats, brother and sister, Jessie and Jack.

In 2010, a few months before the family were due to move to a new home near Darwin, Jack went missing. When he didn't return, Sheree feared the worst and, with a heavy heart, she made the 3,000 km move with just Jessie in tow.

Unfortunately, shortly after, Sheree was to be devastated again when Jessie also went missing.

Meanwhile, the new family who had moved into the farmhouse back in Ungarra had an unexpected visitor: a little tabby cat had arrived on their doorstep. Jenn Humby, the new owner, contacted Sheree and showed her a photograph: it was indeed Jack. He had come home. However, much as Sheree and her family missed Jack, they knew that he would be happier at the farmhouse, so arrangements were made for the new owners to adopt him.

It was 15 months later when Jenn made another remarkable discovery at the farmhouse: a second tabby cat was curled up next to Jack. Astonishingly, it was Jessie. The little cat had made the 3,000 km trip across the outback to find her old home and her brother.

Nobody can truly know what Jessie experienced on that journey but luck was definitely on her side: 2010 was the third wettest year on record for the region, and severe flooding had turned the red Australian deserts green. The treacherous dry landscape was transformed, as the water brought an explosion of insects and animals, including mice, which would have been the perfect snacks for Jessie's journey. Mother Nature was most certainly looking out for her.

Both Sheree and Jenn were overjoyed that brother and sister were reunited and well, and they were amazed by Jessie's epic journey. It was agreed that both cats would be cared for by Jenn at the farmhouse, as that was clearly where they both wanted to be. Jessie's astonishing tale of survival and devotion to her brother makes her a truly remarkable cat.

A PLACE TO CALL HOME

Cats are territorial creatures, and they spend a great deal of time securing their home range. They negotiate access and spraying rights with other cats, so they do not like changes. Most owners, upon moving, will keep their cats indoors for a few weeks until they come to recognise the new house as 'home'.

Cats are also renowned for their homing instincts. They have a heightened sense of smell which can help them to determine which way is home. Some scientists believe that cats have magnetised cells in their brains which act as an internal compass, helping them to sense direction. A cat knows where it wants to live and will use all its powers to get there. So whilst cats have a range of up to 1,500 metres from their house, they will always look to return to the base.

There are many tales of felines who have travelled great distances to get back home. A cat called Pilsbury refused to accept his family's move eight miles away and returned to his old house over 40 times. Although to get there he needed to cross busy roads and fields filled with cattle, Pilsbury was undaunted. Another cat – Ninja – moved with his family from Utah to Washington in the USA but clearly disapproved of the new place and soon decided to show it. Ninja emerged in good health at his former home in Utah just over a year later, having completed the journey of 850 miles.

MRS CHIPPY

A tabby tomcat accompanied the crew of the Endurance *on their ill-fated voyage to cross the Antarctic. The relationship he forged with his owner transcended death...*

Ernest Shackleton and his crew aboard the *Endurance* set sail from London's East India Docks on 1 August 1914, bound for the Antarctic. The crew's aim was to make the first land crossing of the Antarctic continent. In 1911, Norwegian Roald Amundsen had led the first expedition that reached the South Pole, but for Shackleton's crew the crossing of the continent from end to end remained a great challenge.

There were 28 men on board and a tabby cat called Mrs Chippy. Despite the name, Mrs Chippy was a tough tomcat from Glasgow who belonged to the ship's carpenter, Harry McNish. Harry had found the little animal curled up in one of his toolboxes as he was preparing to board the ship. The cat seemed determined to join the crew so Harry decided to take him aboard. A 'chippy' is a slang term for a carpenter and, as the cat followed Harry around the ship like a possessive wife, he got this unusual name, which stuck even when the men discovered that 'she' was in fact a tomcat.

Shackleton was pleased to have the cat on board. Mrs Chippy proved himself to be a good mouse-catcher and helped to prevent rodents from decimating their precious stores. Mrs Chippy was also good-natured and affectionate, and became a firm favourite of most of the crew. The only members who weren't so keen on Mrs Chippy were the 70 sled dogs who had a rather miserable journey chained up in kennels on the deck. Given the important role these animals would later come to play, they were not treated very well and suffered from lack of exercise. Their frustrated howling, at first, frightened and bothered Mrs Chippy but it wasn't long before he realised that he had the upper hand and so would prowl around on top of their kennels, mewling and using the roofs as his own personal scratching posts. Needless to say, the dogs were not fans of Mrs Chippy.

The voyage of the *Endurance* has gone down in history as the last major expedition of the Heroic Age of Antarctic Exploration. It was also a tragic and ill-fated journey. In mid-January 1915 the *Endurance* became trapped in frozen pack ice in the Weddell Sea and those on board were marooned more than 500 km from dry land. Whilst the crew worked to try to release the vessel, Mrs Chippy decided that the best thing to do in the circumstances was to go to ground, and he disappeared for five days at the beginning of January. The crew were distraught, fearing he'd ventured out onto the ice and frozen. So when he finally returned, the men's spirits were lifted.

Mrs Chippy's old adversaries, the dogs, were moved to houses built from the ice so that they could exercise whilst chained to sturdy posts. Mrs Chippy would tempt fate by watching them from just out of range and was accused of deliberately teasing the dogs by an unpopular member of the crew, who threatened to hurt him – he was swiftly demoted. Mrs Chippy did not like the ice and spent much of his time below deck aboard the trapped vessel.

The crew rode out the bitter winter but by February they were still no closer to freeing the vessel, which was being slowly crushed by the powerful ice. Mrs Chippy continued to sleep through much of the drama and one crew member remarked many years later that his feline cool was what kept many of the men going: 'Mrs Chippy's almost total disregard for the diabolical forces at work on the ship was more than remarkable – it was inspirational. Such perfect courage is, alas, not to be found in our modern age.' Many more months passed and by October the *Endurance* was beginning to break up under the pressure. The crew were despondent. Shackleton eventually decided that they needed to abandon ship. They had just three lifeboats and so ruthless decisions needed to be made about what was saved. There was no room, said Shackleton, for any of the sled dogs or for Mrs Chippy.

Harry and the crew were heartbroken but they were unswervingly loyal to Shackleton, so they all said their goodbyes to Mrs Chippy. It is said that Harry took the cat to his tent to say his farewells. A bowl of sardines – Mrs Chippy's favourite – was rustled up and he ate them with relish before falling into a deep sleep. The fish had been laced with a tranquiliser so that the cat would be peaceful when the end came. In his book, *South With Endurance*, Shackleton noted that on the afternoon of 29 October 1915 the cat and some of the dogs were shot.

The crew sailed for Elephant Island in the lifeboats. Harry had no time to mourn his beloved cat but it was said that he had a growing resentment for Shackleton and made no secret of it. Their relationship became strained to the point where Shackleton refused to recommend Harry for a Polar Medal for bravery, despite the fact that it was Harry's carpentry skills that ensured the boats could withstand some of the roughest seas in the world. All the human crew members of the *Endurance* survived, but Harry, who never forgot his beloved cat, couldn't forgive Shackleton for what happened to Mrs Chippy.

In 1925 Harry moved to Wellington, New Zealand, where he worked on the waterfront until he suffered a serious injury, which meant he could no longer work. Harry was close to destitute and only able to survive with help from his neighbours, but even throughout this difficult time, his love for Mrs Chippy remained strong. Baden Norris, the curator of Antarctic History at the museum in Canterbury, recalls meeting Harry when he was old and very ill, and even then mourning the loss of Mrs Chippy. 'The only thing I remember him saying,' recalls Norris, 'was that Shackleton shot his cat.'

When Harry died, he was given a naval funeral. But his grave in the Karori Cemetery remained unmarked until 1959, when the New Zealand Antarctic Society raised a headstone. In 2004 the society cleaned up the grave and commissioned a life-size bronze statue of Mrs Chippy to adorn the grave. Harry's grandson, Tom, who lives in England, was delighted and felt that his grandfather would finally be at peace having been reunited, after a fashion, with his beloved cat. 'I think the cat was more important to him than the Polar Medal,' he said.

TRIM

The first and perhaps the only cat to circumnavigate Australia, Trim was born at sea and belonged to the English explorer Matthew Flinders. His story is one of seafaring adventure and a friendship that has gone down in history...

In 1797, a pregnant cat from Stepney, London, gave birth to kittens a very long way away from home. The cats were on board the HMS *Reliance*, which was sailing somewhere in the South Indian Ocean, between the Cape of Good Hope and Australia's Botany Bay.

Being born at sea meant that the kittens very quickly became used to the movement of the ship. They developed an impressive sense of balance and, unlike most felines, became indifferent to water. One kitten stood out from his brothers and sisters – jet black with a white star on his chest and feet that seemed to have been 'dipped in snow'. He was named Trim by the English explorer Matthew Flinders, after the butler in Laurence Sterne's novel *Tristram Shandy*, because he had 'great fidelity and affection'. Trim was a lively kitten and his activities once led to him falling overboard. Unfazed, the little cat began to swim back towards the ship and when a rope was thrown down to him, Flinders recalls that he 'took hold of it like a man and ran up it like a cat'.

Flinders later wrote an essay titled 'A Biographical Tribute to Trim the Cat'. This piece lay hidden in the archives of the National Maritime Museum for many years before being published in 1973. It is from Flinders's own words that we learn much about Trim and the special relationship they shared:

> *He grew up to be one of the finest animals I ever saw, his tail was long, large and bushy… his head was small and round – his physiognomy bespoke intelligence and confidence – his whiskers were long and graceful and his ears were cropped in a beautiful curve.*

But Trim was not immune to his own charms, wrote Flinders…

> *He was, I am sorry to say, excessively vain of his person, particularly of his snow-white feet. He would frequently place himself on the quarterdeck before the officers, the middle of their walk, and spreading out his two white hands in the posture of the lion couchant would oblige them to stop and admire him.*

Trim was an obliging performer and learned to do many tricks, including jumping over a crew member's clasped hands and lying flat on his back until the order was given to rise. However, it was noted that he would express his impatience with a flick of the tail if the order was a long time coming. According to Flinders, Trim also took an interest in many aspects of the running of the ship. He had a curious fascination with the navigating equipment and when they hoisted the sails, he would climb the rigging faster than any of the men.

Trim was also a star at the captain's table. He would always be the first to arrive for dinner and then wait patiently for each guest to be served their food before politely requesting a morsel from every plate. Most were happy to share their meal but if anyone refused to oblige, Trim would wait until they were distracted or mid-conversation before swiping a piece of meat.

Trim accompanied Flinders on many more voyages. He was with him as he set out to circumnavigate the coastline of Australia, establishing it as a continent and not a collection of islands, as previously thought. Flinders made the circumnavigation again in 1802 and 1803, still accompanied by Trim. The cat was also by Flinders's side when he set sail back to England aboard the *Porpoise*. Unfortunately, the ship hit a coral reef on 17 August 1803 and was wrecked. Flinders, Trim and the rest of the survivors swam ashore to Wreck Reef Bank, where they struggled to survive for two difficult months before being rescued by HMS *Cumberland*.

Unknown to the voyagers, England and France had declared war, so when the ship sailed into port on the French island of Mauritius, Flinders was accused of being a spy and was imprisoned. Unable to look after Trim whilst in jail, Flinders reluctantly arranged for him to be adopted by a local woman and her daughter. Shortly after this, and with his original master still incarcerated, Trim went missing. Flinders was heartbroken and, alas, Trim was never seen or heard from again. Flinders wrote again about his beloved cat:

> To the memory of Trim, the best and most
> illustrious of his race, the most affectionate
> of friends, faithful of servants, and best

of creatures. He made the tour of the globe, and a voyage to Australia, which he circumnavigated, and he was ever the delight and pleasure of his fellow voyagers.

After seven years' imprisonment, Flinders was permitted to leave the island and he set sail for England – on the sea for the first time in years without the company of his beloved cat.

Today neither Flinders nor Trim are forgotten. In 1996 a bronze statue of Trim was created by sculptor John Cornwell and placed on a window ledge of the Mitchell Library in Macquarie Street, Sydney. It stands directly behind the statue of his master, which was erected in 1925. In March 2006, a second statue of Flinders was placed in the marketplace of his hometown of Donington, in Lincolnshire. At his feet is his faithful companion, the cat called Trim.

EMILY

The McElhineys never gave up hope that their beloved cat, Emily, would return, but they never imagined that she could stray quite so far away from home...

Donny and Lesley McElhiney's cat, Emily, was a wanderer. It wasn't the first time she'd gone missing when she disappeared from their home in Appleton, Wisconsin, in September 2005. Following their usual routine, they asked the neighbours, who hadn't seen her, and checked with the local rescue centre. Emily wasn't there either. With heavy hearts, the McElhiney family had to conclude that Emily was lost.

It was around two months later that they received a call from their vet: Emily had been found. Relief swept over the family, followed very swiftly by disbelief. The vet told them that Emily was in France. She had been discovered by workers at a paper lamination factory in Nancy inside a container carrying bales of paper. The container had been packed in Wisconsin, transported across the length of America and then taken by ship across the Atlantic to Belgium, before making the final leg of the journey, back on dry land, to France.

A spokesperson for the paper company, Christèle Gozillon, explained what happened when they discovered the stowaway: 'We received a container from Wisconsin full of bales of adhesive paper. We heard a cat meowing. It was a real surprise. We opened the container gently and a little very frightened cat ran and hid in the lorry engine.' Christèle and her colleagues noticed that the cat was wearing a tag and realised that she must be someone's pet. Emily's collar had a name and address on it and so they were able to contact her vet, John Palarski.

Surviving the journey was no small feat for Emily. She had spent three weeks inside the container and, whilst a cat might find water and mice to catch if they had free rein on a ship, the container had been sealed, and Emily had been trapped. She was weak, thin, thirsty and frightened after her ordeal, but she was alive and about to receive a helping hand getting home.

Emily became known as 'Le Chat Américain' in France. Her story spread throughout the world and won the hearts of management at Continental Airlines. 'This was such a marvellous story, that we wanted to add something to it,' spokesperson Philippe Fleury said to reporters at Charles de Gaulle airport just outside Paris. So, once Emily had cleared her one-month quarantine, she was escorted by Continental Airlines staff member Gaylia McLeod all the way from France back to Wisconsin. Emily flew business class from Paris to Newark, New York, and then from there to Milwaukee. On her flight, Emily passed up a meal of peppered salmon fillet in favour of her new favourite French cat food and a little water. Greeted at the airport by a huge swathe of reporters and her beloved family, Emily returned home a hero. Gaylia had the honour of handing Emily to the McElhiney's nine-year-old son, Nick.

The McElhineys were delighted to have their cat back in their arms. Donny told reporters: 'She'll be held onto a lot all the way home. And then, when we get home she'll be cuddled a lot.'

MR FANCY

A stray cat broke out of an animal shelter just 20 minutes after he was dropped off, and he made his way back to where he belonged...

One spring evening, Anne Bosche was in her garden in Lucedale, Mississippi, when she discovered a stray cat in the bushes. The tabby cat was very frail, and his fur was matted and dirty, but he was friendly. 'What came out from under that bush was a large, beautiful cat with a white tip on his tail,' remembers Anne. 'I said, "Aren't you a fancy thing?"' So the cat became known as Mr Fancy.

Anne offered Mr Fancy some food and water, which he gratefully accepted. He returned the next day and the day after for more. Anne approached her husband to discuss whether the cat could stay with them, as he didn't appear to have any other home to go to and was spending a lot of time in their garden. She was also worried about his health, but Anne's husband was concerned. The couple already had a miniature dachshund and two other cats. Was their house really big enough for another animal? Couldn't this stray find a home at their local shelter? Anne reluctantly agreed.

The next morning the Bosches loaded up Mr Fancy into their cat carrier and drove to the animal shelter. 'I dropped him off,' remembers Anne, 'and an attendant took him to the back where the cages are. When he brought me my carrier back, he said that the cat was back there, banging his head against the iron cage door... I cried the five miles back to my house.'

Anne could not get Mr Fancy off her mind. She was wracked with guilt that she hadn't taken him in and checked the animal shelter's website for the next few days to see if there was an announcement about Mr Fancy being adopted. But there was no news. What Anne didn't know was that the cat had made an audacious and successful escape attempt just 20 minutes after she dropped him off. Meanwhile, people at the shelter were baffled – the cat was nowhere to be found. They could only hope that another good Samaritan like Anne would spot Mr Fancy and return him so that they could ensure he was rehomed. But there was no sign of the cat anywhere. He did not reappear at the shelter – he was gone.

A month later Anne was woken at 5.30 a.m. by the sound of her husband talking to someone in the kitchen. She padded downstairs in her dressing gown to find him standing in the kitchen, staring in wonder at Mr Fancy, who was sitting neatly at his feet. Anne began to cry, as Mr Fancy ran to her. He had found his way back to her and the place he knew was his home.

Mr Fancy must have battled busy streets and rough neighbourhoods to come back to Anne and her husband. 'I think he had a guardian angel looking out for him, directing him back to my house,' she says. 'I love him so much and I feel we were meant to be together. He belongs here. Mr Fancy will never want for a home, food or love again.'

CHAPTER 10

EXTRAORDINARY FELINES

All cats are extraordinary creatures, but in this chapter we will hear the stories of a few particularly special ones. These cats are, by turns, unique, strange, quirky, adventurous, talented, unusual and charming – and just real characters. Some of them have even reached superstar status. Their stories have the ability to capture and delight, and remind us why we, as humans, remain fascinated and enchanted by our feline friends. They are never boring and always unpredictable...

BOB

James Bowen could never have predicted how rescuing an injured ginger stray in 2007 would transform his life and give him back the purpose that he thought he'd lost...

It was 2007 and things were tough for James Bowen. After living for years on the streets of London, he was recovering from a devastating addiction to heroin and scraping a meagre income as a street musician. Now living in a one-bedroom council flat in North London, he was taking each day at a time, clinging to hope and trying to get his life back on track. James had no idea that a cat was about to transform his existence.

It was a cold March morning when a ginger tomcat came into his life. James found the hungry animal in the stairwell of his block of flats and noted that he had a nasty-looking wound to his leg. James felt sorry for the friendly little cat but he didn't feel he was in a position to help another creature: life was a struggle already without an additional mouth to feed. But the cat did not want to leave James. When he saw that it was still there a day or so later, James finally relented and took the cat into his flat for some food. Having checked with his neighbours, James concluded that the cat must be a stray. He took it to his local branch of the RSPCA and spent what little money he had on antibiotics to treat what was diagnosed as an abscess – the cat was going to be OK.

James took the little cat home with him and called him Bob after a character in *Twin Peaks*. Bob recovered over the following weeks and James remained convinced that he would want to move on once he was well again. But the cat had found a soulmate in James. Every day, when James returned from busking, Bob would be waiting for him and soon the cat decided that he really didn't like being without his owner so he tried to go along. James made an effort to persuade him otherwise but eventually Bob became his constant companion: he would travel the London streets perched on James's shoulder and sit by his side as he tried to earn money by playing for the busy city commuters.

The partnership transformed James's life, as having Bob by his side meant that he was no longer 'invisible' on the streets of London. People stopped to chat and take photographs of Bob. The effect on James's takings was also dramatic. He spent some of his earnings on a harness for Bob to keep him safe when they travelled together, a microchip and vaccinations. James started to realise that taking Bob into his home had changed his life entirely and said at the time, 'He's what I wake up for every day now.'

Soon, it became clear to James that he had to find an alternative to busking. He had been warned by the police about performing in places where he shouldn't and he needed to try something else. So, in 2008, James applied to become a *Big Issue* seller. The magazine is published around the world and sold by homeless and long-term unemployed people who can use the profits to get back on the right track. Bob was still by James's side each day and he became hugely popular with regular customers. Their amazing bond was starting to generate interest on social media, where it caught the attention of a literary agent, who could see a great story. She contacted James about writing a book and, in 2012, *A Streetcat Named Bob* was published. Its success was immediate and worldwide, and the book has now been translated into 30 languages and turned into a film. Bob has become a celebrity and regularly appears at signings and on television. In 2013 he attended the British Animal Honours – an event which celebrated the country's most extraordinary animals – where he was awarded the Tails of the Unexpected Honour.

Touched by the public affection for his cat, James wanted to give something back. The Blue Cross had often treated Bob for free when times were tough for the two of them and every year the charity means the difference between life and death for many animals. A campaign launched by James and Bob garnered over £20,000 of donations.

> *The wonderful thing about all this is I have a purpose now. I can help with the Blue Cross, with drug rehabilitation programmes and homelessness programmes. I am able to do all this, just from my voice, just from saving one cat. It's amazing to be able to give back.*

In 2014, it was reported that sales of the books had reached one million – a figure achieved by just a handful of writers. 'It's incredible,' commented James, 'When I first saw Bob on the doorstep I never thought this is where I would be today.'

CLEVER KITTY

Cats are smart. A cat's brain has 1,000 times more 'data storage' than an iPad and operates a million times faster. And although dogs are often considered the smartest domestic pet, cats are in fact just as intelligent but in different ways.

A cat's cerebral cortex contains about twice as many neurons as that of dogs and they have longer-lasting memories. Scientists have also found startling similarities between human and feline brains: cats share a similar brain structure to us with temporal, occipital, frontal and parietal lobes of their cerebral cortex. Each one of these lobes is also connected in the same way as they are in the human brain. Furthermore, the part of the brain that processes emotions works the same in cats as it does in humans.

Dogs, however, do trump their feline friends in social IQ. Cats are far more impulsive and have less patience; they will not tolerate frustrating situations for long, whereas a dog will do almost anything to please its human. A cat will invariably please itself – and why not?

MERLIN

Owners often know that their feline companions are content by the comforting hum of their purr. Thirteen-year-old Merlin makes sure that his message is always loud and clear...

When Tracey Westwood and her daughter Alice headed to their local rescue centre, they hoped to be able to offer a home to a feline friend. They adopted 13-year-old Merlin and he left them in no doubt that he had found his nirvana. Cats often purr when they are content but the Westwoods noticed that Merlin was particularly noisy. They were so bemused by their cat's rowdy purr that they felt they had to share it with the world and so contacted the Guinness World Records. Shortly after his rescue, in 2015, Merlin was confirmed as the cat with the loudest purr in the world.

Merlin's purr was recorded at 67.8 decibels by a World Records adjudicator, beating the previous record holder – another British rescue cat, Smokey – who had registered at 67.68 decibels in 2011. Tracey says:

> *Occasionally, when he's really loud, I have to repeat myself. When you're watching films, you have to turn the telly up or put him out of the room; if he's eating, he'll purr loudly. I can hear him when I'm drying my hair. If he's cleaning, he gets louder and sometimes if the telephone rings, I do get people asking me what's that noise in the background. I tell them it's the cat but I don't know if they believe me.*

Merlin's purr is as noisy as an air conditioner and nearly as loud as a shower or even a dishwasher. 'It was amazing to see how loud his purr was in person,' said Jamie Clarke, official spokesperson for the Guinness World Records, 'and despite a couple of readings of Merlin's purr just under the current record, a bowl of tuna cat food proved to make all the difference and secure the record.'

EDDIE

Vet Karen Horne was carrying out routine vaccinations on a family of kittens when she discovered that one of them was a little miracle...

It was a routine day for vet Karen Horne at her clinic in Harpenden, Hertfordshire. She often worked with local animal welfare charities, and that day she was due to vaccinate a family of four kittens who were in the care of Cat and Kitten Rescue. The little cats were just eight weeks old and they were all beautiful tortoiseshell.

As Karen was checking the health of each of them, she stopped in her tracks. She had noticed something about one of the kittens that couldn't be possible: it was male. As a rule, tortoiseshell cats are always females. This is down to genetics. Every mammal has two sex-determining chromosomes: males have X and Y, whereas females have two X chromosomes. In cats, the X chromosome also carries the genes for tortoiseshell colouring and in order for that to occur, the cat requires two X chromosomes. Male cats only have space for one X chromosome, making it technically impossible for them to inherit the correct combination of genes. But Karen was not mistaken; she held in her hands a male tortoiseshell cat. The odds of this happening were around 400,000 to one.

Karen adopted the kitten and named him Eddie after the cross-dressing comic Eddie Izzard, 'because he is essentially a boy dressed in girls' clothing,' she laughed. Karen already had quite the animal family, with five cats and four dogs, but she couldn't resist Eddie. She didn't tell her long-suffering husband, Mike, about the new addition to the family, but he was soon won over by the kitten. 'My colleagues and I have 30 years of experience between us and we have never seen anything like this,' Karen said. 'I feel like the luckiest vet ever just to see a tortie tomcat, and even luckier to have him live with me. So far there are no signs of any gender confusion and he seems to be all there.'

BARNEY

It's often said that you never own a cat – a cat owns you. A stray kitten with a big personality wandered into the lives of some London residents and ended up ruling the whole street...

It was Halloween in 1996 when Cyndy and David Spicer returned to their home in a quiet street in South London. On the steps of their local corner shop, they found a tiny tabby cat, meowing loudly. Wondering if perhaps he had been spooked by the Halloween festivities, they picked him up and checked with a few neighbours, but nobody knew where the little cat had come from. The family decided to take him home. As the days went by and nobody claimed the tabby, it became clear that he had found a new home and his new family named him Barney. What the Spicers didn't realise was that they hadn't adopted the cat; Barney had adopted them and, as if they weren't enough, he would go on to adopt the entire street.

Barney was a real character. 'Right from the beginning, Barney was nosing into everything,' says Cyndy. 'He was fearless. He had this amazing spirit. He owned the street.' Barney made himself at home in several houses in that road. He was often found snoozing on neighbours' beds and even if they had other cats or dogs, Barney would still make himself welcome. Not content with his comfortable bed at the Spicers' he subsequently found a second home over the road with Colin and Lorraine Wilson. Soon enough, the whole street took a collective responsibility for him and Barney did the same for its residents. He often left little mice tributes on doorsteps or sometimes right at the feet of friends he recognised as they passed him.

Barney didn't limit himself to houses. He was often found at the local primary school where the teachers would share their snacks with him, with crisps being a favourite. Another haunt was the local Tooting and Mitcham Football Club at the bottom of the road, where parties and wedding receptions were often held. Barney would take up station beneath the buffet table until someone noticed a little paw appearing from underneath, snaffling the canapés.

Barney took a turn for the worse in 2010 when he was struck by a car. Although a little wobblier on his legs than before, this didn't stop him from being a real bruiser. Dogs familiar with Barney would often drag their owners across the road to avoid walking past him in his favourite spot, a window box outside the Wilson's living room. He also held his own with the resident South London foxes. Lorraine Wilson recalls him playing with fox cubs early one spring morning, and years later she saw Barney greet an adult fox with a familiar nose bump, as if they were old friends.

Barney passed away in 2015 after 19 years of ruling that street in South London. He is deeply missed by all the residents he stayed with. 'Barney was the ultimate street cat,' explains Cyndy. 'Everybody in the street knew him and welcomed him into their homes. Everybody loved him. I don't think we ever really owned Barney; he owned all of us.'

DO YOU REALLY 'OWN' YOUR CAT?

Cats are very smart, but they are not always loyal. You might think that since you feed your pet, provide them with a warm bed and pay their vets bills that you own them, but it's likely that your cat feels he owns you... and possibly a few of your friendly neighbours too. Many a cat owner has been surprised to walk into a neighbour's house to find their cat enjoying some free hospitality. That's because cats are, by nature, wanderers, explorers and chancers.

Due to their exploratory nature, cats are the only animal exempt from the UK's Animals Act of 1971 which forbids domestic animals from trespassing. Laws stating that dogs must be collared, kept on a lead and controlled by their owners in public places are not applicable to our feline friends. If a dog were to damage a neighbouring garden, the owner would be liable for that damage, but this is not so with cats. They are, in this respect, above the law. This privileged position for cats means that they can clamber uninvited into any garden they wish to visit, much to the annoyance of gardeners throughout the country. This exemption from the law raises a question: can you ever 'own' your cat?

The legal answer is yes. Under the 1968 Theft Act, cats are regarded as the property of the owner so their theft is a prosecutable offence. Likewise, the Criminal Damage Act of 1971 makes it illegal to harm a cat, thus lending further protection to our feline friends. So whilst it might be tempting to claim that 'stray' who visits your garden regularly as your own, every attempt must be made to find the legal owner before a cat is rehomed.

There are also laws that govern the responsibilities of the owner. The 2006 Animal Welfare Act states that owners are legally required to cover all of their cat's needs, including providing a suitable place for them to live, a suitable diet, and protecting them from pain and injury.

ROSIE

When Rosie arrived at her vet for an operation, an amazing discovery was made. Her owner always knew that she was unique but this proved it beyond all doubt...

Darren Smith brought a Maine Coon cross-breed, tabby kitten into his home in Littleport, Cambridgeshire, and called her Rosie. She was a gentle, sweet cat and very affectionate. When Rosie was 15 months old, Darren decided to have her spayed and made arrangements with the local vet, who made an amazing discovery once Rosie was on the operating table: the cat had both male and female genitals.

> *For the past 15 months, since having Rosie from a kitten, I have thought she was this pretty little girl cat and all of a sudden she's both boy and girl.*
>
> *I still see her as a girl but in fact she is more male than female.*
>
> *Obviously, I still love her all the same but I am finding myself looking at her in a different light.*
>
> *But to me she'll always be a girl and I'm certainly not changing her name as that's the name she knows.*

Rosie's vet, Peter Hanlon, confirmed that Rosie was 'more male than female' and as a result she was castrated that day rather than spayed. Peter acknowledged how rare an event this was: 'I've been a vet for more than 20 years and have never come across it before, and from what I gather, not many others have either. Rosie might be unusual but it shouldn't cause her any problems and she should lead a normal, happy and healthy life.' It appears that Rosie truly is one of a kind.

RIGHT-PAWED OR LEFT-PAWED?

Research carried out in 2009 showed that cats have a paw preference, much like left- or right-handedness in humans. The split seems to be on gender lines. Psychologists Deborah Wells and Sarah Millsopp of Queen's University Belfast tested 21 tomcats and 21 female cats to determine whether they preferred using their right or left paws. Three scenarios were used in the testing: in the first, a tempting tuna dish was placed in a narrow-mouthed jar. In the second, a toy mouse was dangled over the cats' heads, and in the third, the toy mouse was dragged across the ground. Each test was repeated 100 times for every cat. In the second and third tests the psychologists noted that the cats used their paws interchangeably. But in the more intricate 'tuna in the jar' test the male cats overwhelmingly used their left paws, whilst the females tended to use their right paws. The findings showed that cats will use a preferred paw for more complex jobs. This mirrors human behaviour, as we use both hands for simple tasks such as opening a door, but for an activity like writing, which requires precision, we use a particular hand. The report also showed that cats mirror humans in another way. Men are more likely to be left-handed than women and it is the same for our feline friends: almost all left-pawed cats are toms and female felines tend to be right-pawed.

MAYOR STUBBS

Holding the position of 'honorary mayor' for 19 years is an achievement for anyone, but there is something very different about Mayor Stubbs...

In the small town of Talkeetna, Alaska, Laurie Stec manages Nagley's General Store. This is the main haunt of Mayor Stubbs, who has held office since 1997.

'He's good. Probably the best we've had,' Laurie says. 'He doesn't raise our taxes, he doesn't interfere with business and he's honest.' Mayor Stubbs's popularity stretches far beyond the borders of his little town. He has more than 70,000 Facebook fans, gets hundreds of letters and receives more than 30 visitors every day, hoping for an audience. Stubbs takes this all in his stride, making sure that he still gets his daily wine glass of water laced with catnip. This is because Mayor Stubbs is a 19-year-old, golden part-Manx cat.

In 1997 Mayor Stubbs, who was then just a kitten, was elected as the figurehead of the town, when the 900 residents rejected all of the human candidates on the ballot paper. Recently, there have even been social media campaigns calling for him to run for President of the United States of America.

Mayor Stubbs also lays claim to some amazing feline survival stories. In August 2013 he was attacked by a dog and injured badly. He's also been shot, fallen into a fryer and recently hitched a ride to the edge of town on a garbage truck.

Skye Farrar, who works with Laurie at Nagley's, says that Mayor Stubbs is a tough boss:

> *All through the day I have to take care of the mayor. He's very demanding. He meowed and meowed and meowed and demanded to be picked up and put on the counter. Then he had his long afternoon nap… You have to deal with it. He runs the town.*

BRIGIT

Six-year-old Tonkinese cat Brigit is a passionate collector. But what she chooses to collect might come as something of a surprise…

Brigit lives in Hamilton, New Zealand, with her owner Sarah Nathan and Sarah's husband. Brigit is an unusual cat: she likes to collect things. In fact, Brigit is so dedicated to her collection that she amassed more than 60 new additions in just under two months. Brigit likes to collect men's underwear.

'In our last house she'd bring us home a bit of everything,' Sarah says. 'She'd bring home men's undies, women's undies, togs... She even brought home a hockey shin pad and a jumper.' Brigit halted her collecting spree for a while when the family moved into their new home in 2016. But she soon picked up her habit again, and with a new focus: Brigit only collects men's garments now.

Preferring to prowl her neighbours' washing lines under cover of darkness, in two months the cat brought home 11 pairs of boxers and more than 50 pairs of socks. She likes to grab socks in pairs, leaving one at the front of her house and one by the back door. Sarah also finds garments that she doesn't recognize in the bedroom, outside Brigit's cat door or even tucked into the fence surrounding their garden. 'It's an absolute obsession,' explains Sarah. 'A night does not go by without her bringing things home.'

Brigit has since posed for a Facebook photo with her haul, which Sarah posted in the hope that some of her neighbours might spot something they thought was missing.

BATMAN

Batman is a very unusual cat with a little something extra...

Cats are said to have nine lives but what about four ears? A three-year-old black cat was brought into the shelter at

Western Pennsylvania Humane Society in Pittsburgh in July 2016. He was suffering from a respiratory infection that needed treatment, but there was something else about him that made the staff take notice: he had four ears.

The cat has a normal set of ears and then two extra flaps behind. Shelter veterinarian Dr Todd Blauvelt said, 'It doesn't really affect his hearing. He can hear just fine.' While in their care as he recovered from his respiratory infection, the staff named the cat Batman.

The unusual ear count is believed to be the result of a recessive gene so although it isn't unheard of, it is very rare. The earliest cat reported as having four ears is Toots, who lived in Ohio in 1938. More recently, Chicago residents Valerie and Ted Rock adopted Yoda – a cat with four ears – in 2008. Yoda was part of a large litter and was the only one among his siblings to have the gift of extra ears.

Once Batman fully recovered, he was put up for adoption and hit the headlines around the world. His newfound celebrity status paid off: after just a few hours, he had found a home. A mother and her young daughter had come forward to adopt him. 'It was fitting because the little girl liked superheroes,' said Caitlin Lasky, marketing communications manager for the Humane Society. Batman is nothing if not a superhero.

ANTONIO

*A gentle tabby called Antonio has a special role in his town
and is a true hero for fellow cats in need...*

Antonio didn't have the best start in life. He was abandoned,
along with his four siblings, when they were just tiny kittens.
Fortunately, the little family was rescued by The Mayhew, an
animal welfare organisation in London, and rehomed. And
so it was that in 2013 Antonio and his sister Serafina went
to live with Sandra.

A few months later, when the kittens had settled in, Sandra's
local vet contacted her to ask whether she'd be happy for
Antonio to take on a special role in the community. As he
was such a gentle, sweet-natured cat, the vet felt that he
would be the ideal candidate to become a feline blood donor.
Sandra agreed and whilst testing Antonio's blood, they made
a wonderful discovery. Sandra had always known that her
boy was special but the vet discovered that he was blood
type B, which is very rare.

Giving blood is entirely harmless for a cat and they are
sedated throughout the procedure to ensure that they are not
distressed. After his first donation, Sarah Eagleton at Village
Vet said, 'He was a little trooper, sat completely still and
wasn't angry with us at all. He was a perfect little donor.'

When another cat fell three storeys from her flat, she was
rushed in for medical attention. She had internal bleeding and
needed an urgent transfusion in order to survive. Antonio
came to the rescue and his donation saved her life. When he
returned home to Sandra that evening, she said that he was

absolutely fine and was just missing a few patches of fur that had been shaved. 'He looks a bit like a lion now actually, with a shaved bit under his chin,' commented Sandra, who was glad to have Antonio home.

BLOOD DONOR CATS

Just like their human carers, cats can need emergency blood transfusions to deal with a number of medical complications. Without the availability of donated blood, vets would not be able to carry out life-saving operations. For humans, the NHS Blood Transfusion Service ensures a steady supply of donated blood. Vets have to rely on their own resources, which is why the Animal Blood Register was created. Accredited vets can sign up to it and search for viable donors when they have a cat in trouble. Owners can register their own cats as potential donors, so when an emergency occurs, vets can contact them and organise a life-saving transfusion. Any cat can be registered as a blood donor. The Animal Blood Register is completely free to use and is a not–for–profit organisation helped by sponsorship and gifts from well-wishers.

CHARLIE

Charlie didn't wait to be let in through the front door like an average cat. He perfected a method to get into his first-floor flat without all that waiting around...

Hannah Smith discovered that her cat Charlie had an extraordinary talent when she let him out of the shared front door of their block of flats only to have him appear on their first-floor balcony moments later.

Hannah had taken Charlie home when he was just a kitten. 'Out of the litter he was the one that looked most mischievous and I liked that about him,' she said. Charlie certainly lived up to those expectations. At the age of seven Charlie had grown tired of always waiting for a passing human to open the door to the block and had taken matters into his own paws. He had learned how to scale the 13-foot roughcast wall at the rear of the building and hop onto Hannah's balcony, where he could meow loudly until he was granted admission.

This became a regular habit and Hannah nicknamed him 'Spider Cat'. Cats are exceptional climbers but scaling such a high vertical wall showed particular skill and determination. Beth Skillings, a veterinary officer with the charity Cats Protection, said, 'It's unusual to see a cat scaling such a high wall. He must have very strong claws.'

Charlie's fellow feline roommates, Denny and Falkirk, don't seem to share his taste for gravity-defying antics and prefer to watch him from the balcony as he performs his amazing feats.

ALMOND

Almond was born in a tree and he wasn't going to leave it until gravity gave him a helping hand. Fortunately, he had a human carer around to help him out...

In the hollow of a maple tree in Wisconsin, local resident Ron Venden made a cosy dwelling for a cat called Almond. He built him platforms and little decks within the tree, and returned each day to feed him. Almond had been born in the tree but when his mother left with all his brothers and sisters, leaving him behind, he was alone. Ron had tried to coax the cat down but Almond was having none of it. So Ron, a retired carpenter, decided to make him as comfortable as possible. In fact, Almond was so comfortable that he refused to move.

Ron was convinced that Almond was staying in the tree, as he could never see any paw prints around the trunk when it snowed and locals had never seen the cat with his feet on the ground. Every day Ron would climb up a 12-foot ladder to check on him and feed him. Almond had a protected straw bed in the hollow of the tree, as well as dry cat food to snack on between the fresh meals that Ron delivered.

'I've tried to bring him down a couple of times and he starts scratching.' Ron explained. 'The neighbours think I'm goofy.' When asked why he thought Almond chose the arboreal life, he chuckled, 'I think it's because I'm treating him too good.' Indeed, Almond did not seem to be in a hurry to leave his luxury tree house. Even in single-digit temperatures, he sat proudly in his thick fur coat, surveying the world from his perch.

But in 2011 Almond took a tumble. Ron found him at the bottom of his tree with a broken leg. Almond had fallen 13 feet and needed extensive surgery. 'I had built some little decks for him to lay on with carpet,' said Ron. 'Whether he was sleeping and just rolled off I don't know. I should have had a safety rail on there I suppose.' Fortunately for Almond, he had his special friend Ron on hand to help him out again. Perhaps now he will keep his four feet firmly on the ground.

TREE DWELLER OR BUSH DWELLER?

Wendy Hobbs spotted a tortoiseshell cat in a tree in her garden in Reepham, Norfolk. She managed to coax the animal down with some food but, after eating, the cat decided to resume her position and hopped straight back up in her tree. She stayed there for some weeks, only hitting the ground to eat.

Cats are excellent climbers and jumpers, but they are equally at home closer to the ground, as they hunt their prey or play with toys. It's important that cats have an environment where they can express these behavioural needs.

Cat behaviourist Jackson Galaxy has presented the theory of 'bush dwellers' and 'tree dwellers' The latter need vertical space. These are the cats that like to jump onto counters, onto the tops of chairs and onto shelves – or perhaps you will find them climbing the curtains. A 'bush dweller' tends to seek out lower spaces like those underneath tables or beds. Galaxy believes that by understanding your cat's preference, you can create environments that work for them and keep them stimulated and happy. 'Tree dwellers' will love to spend time hanging out on a cat tree and prefer a tall scratching post, whilst a tunnel or a covered bed are ideal for your 'bush dweller' cat. Galaxy also points out that many cats, whilst having an obvious preference, will indulge in a little of both.

NORA

It was love at first sight when Betsy Alexander met Nora. What she didn't realise was that her little cat would win the hearts of people around the world with her passion…

Betsy Alexander and her husband Burnell were out shopping for cat food for their five cats in their hometown of Cherry Hill, New Jersey. On these trips, the couple often liked to have a look at the cats awaiting new homes at their local shelter. There were a lot of felines scampering about and playing that day, but when Betsy laid eyes on a little cat playing all by herself, she felt a tug on her heartstrings.

Betsy bent down and scooped her up, and the cat started to play with her long braid. That was all it took: they had a new member of the family.

A few days later, Betsy returned to collect her new pet and bring her home. As she wandered up and down the rows of cages, she saw that all of them had been labelled with details about the cats' personalities. Some said: 'Good with children', while others stated: 'Likes dogs'. The label on the cage of her new charge was 'BOSSY'. But Betsy would not be swayed: this cat was coming home with her.

She was named Nora, after the artist Leonora Carrington, and soon started living up to the description that the shelter had written on her cage. It wasn't long before she was ruling the house and her fellow felines. Betsy is a piano instructor and Nora liked to watch her teach, following the lessons with careful consideration. She especially liked the sound of the Alexanders' grand pianos and would sit underneath during lessons to appreciate the music at full volume.

It was when Nora was one year old that she truly embraced her musical side. One day Betsy watched as the cat clambered up onto the stool in front of her favourite grand piano, tentatively reached out a paw and began to press the keys. Just like humans, she could make music and she was hooked. She liked the high notes more than the low notes and started experimenting with volume. The cat began playing alongside her owner every day and, encouraged by her students, Betsy filmed Nora and put it on YouTube in 2007. The effect was immediate. The video was watched more than 17 million times and Nora became world famous. Soon the clip was being shown on talk shows around the world hosted by famous names like Tyra Banks, Ellen DeGeneres, Martha Stewart and many more. Nora was even called in to do a live performance on *The Today Show* to silence some of the critics who thought the video was fabricated. 'This is her own thing; it's not a trick,' said Betsy. 'It's not something we taught her.'

Although Nora seems to enjoy the fuss she gets when she makes her music, Betsy believes that she plays ultimately for herself. 'She plays when we're not in the room; she plays when we're in the room; sometimes she plays when we don't want her to play. I can be teaching a child or an adult who is trying to concentrate and then Nora hops on the bench.'

Nora is now an international media star: she has her own blog, her own DVD and a book called *Nora the Piano Cat's Guide to Becoming a Good Musician*. Betsy has also written a composition called 'Fur Release: A Prelude for Paws and Hands', which incorporates Nora's music. A CD with a song featuring the cat playing has also been released by the Laurel Canyon Animal Company.

OSCAR

A fluffy grey-and-white cat called Oscar adopted by a nursing home in Rhode Island possesses a rather unusual ability...

Steere House Nursing and Rehabilitation Centre in Providence, Rhode Island, is home to a cat called Oscar. He was brought there as a kitten along with six other cats who were adopted to provide pet therapy to the home's residents. Oscar was a particularly fickle feline and wasn't always friendly. He would often sniff the air of a resident's room and, detecting something not to his taste, turn his tail and continue on his rounds. On other occasions Oscar would be found curled up on the bed next to a patient who had been shunned the day before. It wasn't long before doctors started to notice a pattern to Oscar's behaviour. Whenever a resident passed away, Oscar was present. Could Oscar predict when people were going to die?

Dr Joan Teno of Brown University became convinced – after witnessing the little cat on the deathbed of 13 of her patients – that Oscar had a sixth sense. One day she was tending to a patient who had taken a turn for the worse. As she had stopped eating and her breathing was difficult, Joan was convinced that her time was near. So she was surprised to see Oscar stop at the door, give a quick sniff and then continue on his rounds. Had the cat lost his touch? Was his presence at the deaths of all the other residents just a coincidence? It turned out that Dr Teno had been a bit hasty. The lady passed away peacefully, with Oscar curled up next to her on the bed where he had been for two hours, ten hours later.

By the time he was two years old, Oscar had 'predicted' the deaths of 25 residents at Steere House. After his arrival, it was often half a day – or even just three or four hours – before the patient breathed their last. Oscar's accuracy means that staff are able to contact families of patients so that they have time to say goodbye to their loved ones. Most people are thankful for the presence of Oscar and the early warning he gives them – they see him as a friendly messenger rather than a harbinger of death – and only one patient has had family who preferred to say goodbye without the cat there.

'They appreciate the companionship that Oscar provides for their dying loved ones,' says Dr David Dosa, a geriatrician at Steere House. Oscar usually remains with the residents until the undertaker arrives, and he then attends the funeral procession to the door.

Dr Dosa became involved with a study published by the New England Journal of Medicine about this extraordinary cat. 'Oscar seems to understand when patients are about to die,' he said. They wanted to try to find out how. One suggestion was that, having grown up in the nursing home, Oscar could have become attuned to the various signs of oncoming death – but none of his other feline friends ever exhibited his special ability. Another was that Oscar noticed a change in the behaviour of the staff towards patients whose health was deteriorating, but Dr Dosa pointed out that this would not account for the cases where staff were taken by surprise. Another hypothesis was that Oscar is very sensitive to the scents, chemicals and hormonal changes in the body that happen before death – changes that are imperceptible to humans. Research shows that cats are able to identify the presence of cancer, oncoming seizures and low blood sugar in humans, so this is one of the most plausible explanations.

However, Oscar's predisposition to stay by the patients' side once he's made his prediction cannot be explained. Dr Teno says:

> He's not a bad omen. He comforts the
> dying patients – and what's striking is that,
> in a centre that offers a real gold-standard
> in end-of-life treatment, Oscar seems to be
> mimicking the behaviour of those who work
> there. He makes the room feel like more of

a homely setting and has become part of the
soothing ritual.

Oscar's story has been told all over the world and the staff at Steere House have received hundreds of letters from people claiming to know cats who have displayed similar abilities to Oscar's.

THE ACRO-CATS

A group of cats is taking the world of show business by storm, reinventing what it means to be a feline and doing their bit for cat welfare along the way...

Samantha Martin doesn't believe in the old adage: 'You can't train a cat.' Indeed, she's proved it wrong more than a dozen times. Samantha is the creator and chief cat trainer at The Amazing Acro-Cats, a highly successful live show based in Chicago. Of her 15 performing cats, all but two are female, and they are mainly orphans, rescues and strays. Samantha and her troupe of felines tour the USA for months at a time on a bus known as the cat-mobile. The Acro-Cats perform on a nightly basis for packed-out audiences: they jump, they dance and they play instruments – almost like a live version of YouTube. The show's grand finale is a performance from a feline rock band, The Rock Cats. The cats have even welcomed other species into the troupe: Cluck Norris the chicken and Garfield the groundhog.

Samantha uses clicker training to teach the cats to perform tricks. A treat is given at the sound of a click at the exact moment when the cat is behaving as desired. 'It's more of a fine-tuning way of training,' Samantha explains. 'It's noise and treats. It triggers something in their brain, and they get it very quickly.' But cats being cats, it doesn't always work: sometimes they will decide that they don't want to perform and just wander off to investigate the audience. 'But that's fun too,' says Samantha.

The Acro-Cats aren't all about the bright lights of fame and show business, though. Samantha aims to promote the welfare and the public perception of cats. 'We use our show as an entertaining demonstration of what cats are really capable of, as well as the healthy benefits of clicker training.' She believes that this method can build stronger relationships between owners and their cats, and could be crucial when emergency situations demand immediate action. For example, cats can be trained to climb into their carrier at the sound of a whistle. It can help to solve and prevent behavioural problems, and also provides mental stimulation and physical exercise for the animal.

Samantha and the Acro-Cats also tour with a cat crèche on board the cat-mobile. This is made up of a group of foster cats who are all in need of new homes. Samantha gives them basic clicker training and audience members can then apply to adopt them. So far, Samantha has rehomed 158 cats whilst on tour and, as if that wasn't enough, the Acro-Cats donate a portion of their takings to local rescue centres and have also put on benefits for specific animal welfare organisations.

But all this good work wouldn't be possible without Samantha's extraordinary cats: Alley, Asti, Annie, Buggles,

Buffy, Dakota, Jax, Nola, Nue, Pinky, Pudge, Oz, Wiki, Sookie and Tuna – they are the real stars.

PUTTING ON
A SHOW

Unlike dogs, cats are not perceived as being receptive to training. However, as they are very observant, cats are actually much quicker at learning tricks than their canine counterparts. A cat will watch their owner open the door to the garden a number of times before realising that a quick jump and a pull on the handle mean they can let themselves out. Likewise, you might find your cat scratching intently at the lock on their cat flap, knowing that something there has to happen. Cats often figure out which behaviours will get their owner's attention: a certain sound or a quick scratch on a precious piece of furniture will often do the trick if they feel they are being ignored.

Historical examples of performing animals have often been revealed as unnecessarily cruel, especially by our modern standards of animal welfare. However, Samantha's click training methods are generally thought of as harmless and engaging for the cats. And of course, Samantha is quite used to her performers completely ignoring commands when the mood takes them. They are, after all, cats and they will do what they want.

ACKNOWLEDGEMENTS

I love cats and I thought I knew a lot about them, but researching this book has taught me so much more about our feline friends. They are smart, loyal, caring, brave and amazing creatures. I have read stories that have made me cry, made me laugh and made me thankful that I live in a world with cats. But cats need us to tell their stories. Every tale within this book has a cat at its heart but it also has an extraordinary human being whose life has been changed – and for the better.

Thanks go to Louise Waters and Zahir White of Cats Protection for sharing the stories of Prince Smokey, Spike, Jessie, Gemini, Mr Brutus, Frank, Smokie and Tink on behalf of their owners. Thanks to Cyndy Spicer and Lorraine Wilson for sharing Barney's story with me, and to Sebastian Smetham for Luigi's story. Thanks also to everyone who continues to tell their cats' amazing tales online and in the media. And, finally, thanks to Tommy, my own rescued super cat.

USEFUL RESOURCES AND INFORMATION

Battersea Dogs and Cats Home

For over 150 years Battersea Dogs and Cats Home have been caring for abandoned animals and reuniting lost pets with their owners. The aim of the organisation is to never turn an animal away, caring for them until they find their owners or new homes. Every year 8,000 animals come through their doors. It's a great place to look if you are considering adopting a cat and need advice. They are also grateful for donations.

www.battersea.org.uk

Cat Blood Donors

A free-to-use online registry to bring animal blood donors to the attention of vets so that lives can be saved. Every day cats need blood transfusions, which can in many cases be life-saving. This website allows veterinary practices to contact the owners of cats listed as potential donors in emergency situations. You can register your cat for free on the website. Blood donation is painless and safe for cats.

www.catblooddonors.com

Cat Chat - The Cat Rescue Resource

Launched in 2000 by Mandy and Steve, inspired and assisted by their two rescue cats Gemini and George, this web-based charity works with rescue shelters across Britain and Ireland to find homes for cats. Their website offers 'Virtual Cat Shelters' and lots of advice on caring for our feline friends.

www.catchat.org

Cats Protection

From humble beginnings in 1927, Cats Protection is now the leading feline welfare charity. They help around 200,000 cats and kittens every year through their nationwide network of 250 volunteer-run branches and adoption centres. Their website is full of advice and information. Their vision is a world where every cat is treated with kindness and respect, and they work tirelessly to campaign for legislation to protect cats.

www.cats.org.uk

The Cat Site

Delve into articles on a range of feline issues covering health, behaviour and food. Register to use the lively forums and chat to fellow cat owners about your concerns or just share your stories about your own little ball of purr.

www.thecatsite.com

Celia Hammond Animal Trust

Born out of Celia's love of animals and her concerns for the rising feral population of cats in London, this award-winning charity is responsible for establishing two clinics in the capital which offer vaccinations and neutering, as well as a rescue service for animals. They have also established a sanctuary in Hastings where they care for abandoned animals and work to find new homes for them.

www.celiahammond.org

Crafty Cat

An invaluable and fascinating online resource on feline psychology. Ideal for owners looking to understand their cat's behaviour or for cat lovers to find out more about felines. Crafty Cat also offers a range of vintage cat postcards and digital downloads.

www.craftycat.co.uk

The Governing Council of the Cat Fancy

The premier registration body for cats in the UK – essentially, the feline equivalent of the Kennel Club. Their website offers information on breeding and choosing the right type of cat for your circumstances and lifestyle, as well as advice on the specific needs of certain breeds. The GCCF has a strategic role in protecting the health and welfare of cats and works with major organisations in the UK.

www.gccfcats.org

International Cat Care

Established over 50 years ago as The Feline Advisory Bureau (FAB) and now renamed International Cat Care, this organisation has been raising the standard of treatment and care provided to cats by veterinary surgeons, boarding cattery operators, those involved in rescue work, breeders and cat owners by providing the best information possible. Their website features invaluable and trustworthy advice on caring for your cat or kitten.

www.icatcare.org

The Mayhew Animal Home

One of the most effective animal welfare organisations in London, it helps thousands of dogs and cats every year to escape lives of abandonment and cruelty. The Mayhew can house around 30 dogs and 150 cats and kittens. They run a foster care programme, and offer low-cost neutering and vaccinations. They also run a Pet Refuge Scheme for owners in crisis, allowing them to place their animals in a safe and caring home for a short period of time. The Mayhew is entirely funded by public donations.

www.themayhew.org

Moggies - Home of the Online Cat Guide

Comprehensive advice on caring for your cat from before birth into their old age, including information on feeding, exercise and play, basic first aid, and common ailments.

www.moggies.co.uk

PDSA

Founded by Maria Dickin in 1917, The People's Dispensary for Sick Animals provides free veterinary treatment to over 470,000 much loved animals whose owners cannot afford it. They believe that pets are part of the family and they don't deserve to suffer through economic and social hardship. They also run the PDSA Awards, which recognise acts of extraordinary animal bravery or exceptional devotion.

www.pdsa.org.uk

Pets As Therapy

Founded in 1983, Pets As Therapy organise visits of trusted volunteers and their behaviourally assessed animals to hospitals, hospices, nursing and care homes, special needs schools and many other venues across the UK. They firmly believe that the company of cats and dogs can be of great benefit to the lives of people suffering from debilitating mental and physical health conditions.

www.petsastherapy.org

Purr 'n' Fur

'There's no such thing as too many cats' it says on the opening page of this fantastic website about everything feline: a lovingly curated collection of stories about famous cats, remarkable moggies, humans who've gone the extra mile to help their feline friends, and recommended reading. Purrfect for any cat lover to while away a few hours...

www.purr-n-fur.org.uk

Scottish SPCA – Scotland's Animal Welfare Charity

Established in 1839, the SPCA is Scotland's major animal welfare charity. They rescue animals in danger, find new homes for them, investigate claims of abuse and prevent cruelty through their free Prevention through Education programme for Scottish schools.

www.scottishspca.org

Start A Cattery

An excellent resource for anyone considering running their own cattery or working in an existing one. Advice is available on all aspects of the business from choosing a site, financing, adhering to regulations, staffing, supplies and, of course, caring for your feline guests.

www.startacattery.co.uk

WONDER
DOGS

TRUE STORIES
of CANINE COURAGE

BEN HOLT

WONDER DOGS
True Stories of Canine Courage

Ben Holt

£8.99

Paperback

ISBN: 978-1-84953-997-5

Meet the Super Dogs:

Daisy, the tiny Dachshund who put her life on the line to save her humans from a bear.

Charco, the veteran sniffer dog who has saved countless human lives, and yet still keeps his tail wagging.

Delta, the dog who died trying to protect her young owner from a volcano – after already having saved his life three times.

It's a truth universally acknowledged that dogs are pretty great. But when it comes to facing peril, these loyal creatures always seem willing to step up to the mark and become true doggy heroes. Whether they're saving humans from dangerous people or situations, helping those who are ill, fighting crime or just following their animal instincts to do good, the true stories collected in this book prove that dogs aren't only man's best friend – they're also inspirational, courageous and selfless companions.

ANIMAL
HEROES

True Stories of
Extraordinary Creatures

Ben Holt

ANIMAL HEROES
True Stories of Extraordinary Creatures

Ben Holt

£8.99

Paperback

ISBN: 978-1-78685-005-8

Magic, the miniature pony who helped a woman speak again after three years of silence.

Stubby, the stray dog who braved the front line with soldiers in World War One.

Moko, the bottlenose dolphin who guided a mother whale and her calf back out to sea.

No matter how cute and cuddly our animal companions are, there are always occasions when they remind us that they're still in touch with their natural instincts. Sometimes this comes as little gestures of loyalty, and other times they do something that is truly amazing – even saving human lives.

Animal Heroes contains some of the most extraordinary true tales of bravery across the natural world, from domestic pets to wild animals, proving that when it comes to facing danger there's more to them than meets the eye.

CATS

A MISCELLANY

ANNA MARIA ESPSÄTER

CATS
A Miscellany

Anna Maria Espsäter

£9.99

Hardback

ISBN: 978-1-84953-735-3

*'There are few things in life
more heart-warming than being
welcomed by a cat.'*
Tay Hohoff

'The smallest feline is a masterpiece.'
Leonardo da Vinci

This pocket-sized miscellany, packed with fascinating facts, heart-warming stories and inspiring quotes about cats, is perfect for anyone who knows the incomparable joy of hearing the soothing purr of a feline companion.

Oscar
the Bionic Cat

A Heart-Warming Tale of Feline Bravery

Kate Allan

OSCAR: THE BIONIC CAT
A Heart-Warming Tale of Feline Bravery

Kate Allan

£8.99

Paperback

ISBN: 978-1-84953-380-5

When Kate Allan's beloved black cat, Oscar, is found lying severely injured in a field near their Jersey home, she is sure the accident-prone boy has met his end. With both hind legs severed by a combine-harvester, his life hangs in the balance; luckily for Oscar, his vet knows Noel Fitzpatrick, star of Channel 4's *The Supervet*, who agrees to try pioneering surgery to replace his legs with specially created prosthetics.

This is the amazing true account of a loving family faced with agonising decisions and unexpected twists of fate, and a courageous black feline destined to become the world's first bionic cat.

Have you enjoyed this book?
If so, why not write a review on your
favourite website?

If you're interested in finding out more
about our books, find us on Facebook
at **Summersdale Publishers** and
follow us on Twitter at **@Summersdale**.

Thanks very much for buying this
Summersdale book.

www.summersdale.com